The Field

to

Ocean Voyaging

Animals, Ships, and Weather at Sea

Ed Sobey, Ph.D.

SEAWORTHY PUBLICATIONS, INC. • MELBOURNE, FLORIDA

The Field Guide to Ocean Voyaging
Animals, Ships, and Weather at Sea

ISBN 978-1-948494-02-1

Published in the USA by:
Seaworthy Publications, Inc.
6300 N. Wickham Rd., 130-416
Melbourne, Florida 32940
Phone 310-610-3634
email orders@seaworthy.com
www.seaworthy.com

Library of Congress Cataloging-in-Publication Data

Names: Sobey, Edwin J. C., 1948- author.
Title: The field guide to ocean voyaging : animals, ships, and weather at sea
  / Ed Sobey.
Description: Melbourne, Florida : Seaworthy Publications, Inc., [2018] |
  Includes index.
Identifiers: LCCN 2018006772 (print) | LCCN 2018024645 (ebook) | ISBN
  9781948494038 (epub) | ISBN 1948494035 (epub) | ISBN 9781948494021
(pbk. :
  alk. paper) | ISBN 1948494027 (pbk. : alk. paper)
Subjects: LCSH: Ocean travel--Guidebooks. | Sailing--Guidebooks.
Classification: LCC G550 (ebook) | LCC G550 .S63 2018 (print) | DDC
  910.4/5--dc23
LC record available at https://lccn.loc.gov/2018006772

Acknowledgments

FRIENDS I'VE MET ON SEMESTER AT SEA AND ON commercial cruise ships have provided many of the photos. Will Hayes let me use some of his wonderful shots. He invites people interested in his photos to contact him at wchayes142@gmail.com.

Charles Ford has traveled extensively and has a huge life list of birds. He provided some spectacular shots ranging from the tropics to Antarctica.

Bill Yeaton, Dr. Bill on Semester at Sea, has an extensive collection of photos from his travels. You can view them at his site: www.billyeaton.com.

Another veteran of Semester at Sea is Ryan Bent. He is one of the official photographers for their voyages. He displays his work at www.ryanbent.com.

Rob Avery is an expert kayak instructor and explorer of the world. He paddles in the Aleutian Islands and British Columbia. Somehow at the critical moment he manages to drop his paddle, extract his camera from its waterproof case, and snap beautiful photos. He is the juggling photographer of the high seas.

Running and hiking partner Rod Brown has accompanied us on voyages. Luckily for me he had his camera when I did not.

Sally Mizrock and Carol Ladd travel thousands of miles aboard NOAA research ships in the Bering and Chukchi Seas. Sally is a Vancouver Award winner from the Pacific Northwest Chapter of the Explorers Club. Carol is a long-distance runner and kayaker when she is not working as a research oceanographer for NOAA.

Captain Rick Fehst captains crabbing and fishing boats out of Dutch Harbor, Alaska. We met on Semester at Sea where we gave some joint lectures to students. Rick knows fishing and the ocean having spent many years at sea in a small boat.

We've sailed across the Pacific Ocean together and traveled throughout the world. For nearly 50 years Barbara and I have shared adventures. She took a lot of the photos in this book.

Thank you all for contributing.

The Gangway

CURIOUS CRUISERS, WELCOME ABOARD. WHETHER you are sailing aboard a friend's yacht or a cruise ship, your passage offers the opportunity to see wonders of the sea. Your observational persistence and this book will make your voyage more enjoyable. Your persistence will keep you looking when others leave the deck. This book will guide you to see more and understand what you see at sea.

My ocean experience spans duty as a naval officer aboard a survey ship and as a research oceanographer on several other research ships. I've recorded whale vocalizations in Alaska from an ocean kayak and completed several circumnavigations as a professor with *Semester at Sea.* I speak on commercial cruise ships and SCUBA dive around the world in my quest to see the wonders of the ocean. I spent six weeks living on sea ice in an Antarctic research project and have sailed across the Pacific Ocean in a 54' ketch. If you and I sail together you'll find me on deck looking out at the ocean with a sense of awe, wonder, and hope.

I am fascinated by what I see, and I hope you will be too. Have a wonderful voyage.

Table of Contents

Chapter 1

Before You Go

Which Cruise?

SINCE YOUR EYES ARE SCANNING THIS PAGE I assume you are planning to spend time at sea and want to see the wonders of the sea. Here are some suggestions for picking the cruise that will best suite your interests.

Opportunities for marine sightings

Some itineraries provide more opportunities to see the natural and technical marvels of the ocean. Obviously if your ship is docking every morning at dawn and leaving every evening at sunset you won't see much. Sea days are what you need.

Some of the smaller cruise ships will slow down or stop so you can see whales or other wildlife. They might make announcements on the deck to alert you to the sightings. Larger ships generally will not.

Trans-oceanic crossings offer the most sea days. Many people think they offer too many sea days. But often the price is right. Unfortunately on many of those sea days the ship will be far from sea lanes and far from the animals you want to see.

As a general rule, the most interesting routes overlap whale migrations or include coastal areas where marine life flourishes. Searching for day excursions in each port of call will reveal if whales, seals, birds, or other wildlife are present. Check the seasonality as many marine animals migrate and may be seen only in some months. See our specific recommendations for areas to see whales.

Excursions

Check the itinerary and the excursions that are offered. They tell you what their passengers expect. In the few hours of a typical port call you can't get far into the interior. Some port calls include two nights, but not many.

If there are no excursions for whale and dolphin watching, there probably aren't any whales or dolphins in the area at that time of year. Same for viewing birds. Read the description carefully as some tour operators will suggest you can see wildlife without mentioning seasonal variability.

Shore excursions tend to follow a pattern: bus trip to some site, lunch, stops at souvenir shops, and back to the ship. The souvenir shops are often camouflaged as artisan workshops or plantations or rug factories. Most excursions involve people climbing on and off a big bus. If you're good with this format, you will have a lot to choose from.

If you want to explore the natural environment or understand the local culture, you'll have to dig through the offerings to find excursions that will interest you. Check the level of physical activity to see if it is right for you.

Understand that cruise ship companies make much of their profit by offering excursions. You can do at least as well or much better by creating your own tour. Check the internet to see what is offered. You may find a local tour provider who offers you the same or better tour for not much more than the ship would charge. If you have a particular passion that you want to pursue in each port, unless the cruise includes that theme you'd be better off finding your own excursions.

I find it less stressful to make arrangements in advance. It's nice to have someone holding a sign with your name on it when you disembark. But when I haven't done my homework or found a reasonable price, we walk off the ship to talk to the drivers who are standing at the port entrance. Usually for the same price you would pay for the ship's tour you can get local transportation for a tour of your own design. The plus is that you will see more and spend less time waiting for other people to re-board the bus, and avoid the places you'd just as soon not visit. The balance is that you have

Sailing through a narrow passage makes for dramatic scenery. Every bend brings new things to see. In Norwegian fjords, you see small communities every few minutes that are tucked away inside bays.

In Dakar, Senegal we negotiated a great price with a driver and off we went in his car. A few blocks later he asked for some money for gas. I was hesitant and said it had to come out of the total price we had agreed to. He said no, it was extra. We turned around so he could drop us back at the taxi gathering spot outside the port gates. We started the negotiating process again.

The second driver, older and shrewder, agree to the price and down the road we went, again. After 30 minutes or so he pulled over. He had to get a police pass, he said, to enter the next section of the country and the cost was $10. I paid, he went inside a building and came out a few minutes later. He had a piece of paper in his hand that he showed me, saying it was the pass. When we returned to Dakar three days with a different driver, no police pass was required. He scammed me.

to negotiate and have confidence in yourself to get back to the ship before sailing in case the driver turns out to be a flake. In countries with robust economies drivers and cars will be much more expensive: Sweden or Norway for example. In countries with weaker economies renting a car and driver can be inexpensive.

We've never had the problem arranging our own. We don't pay the drivers until they drop us off at the dock and they will do whatever it takes to make us happy enough to pay them.

All that said, you may find the ship's excursions the best or at least easiest way to go. They take care of you, ensure you're back on the ship before sailing, and make all the arrangements.

The drivers who are soliciting business inside the port have to pay for that privilege. That means you pay for that privilege. If you walk out of the port entrance you will likely find another group of drivers who will charge less. Walk farther into town, assuming there is a town next to the port, and the price might drop more.

One more suggestion with hiring drivers. Check out the driver, his or her language skills, and check out the vehicle. Recently I made a deal to hire a driver in Bulgaria without looking at his car. As we got into the car we saw it had clear plastic tape for a rear window that fluttered noisily as we drove down the highway.

All-inclusive, or pay as you go

The waiter is re-filling your wine glass without you asking him. In fact, you have to tell him to stop when you've had enough. Welcome to the all-inclusive cruises.

With all-inclusive cruises you are not constantly digging out your ship's ID to pay. Lattes, wine, and other drinks are all included. You might think people would take advantage of this to extremes, but not so usually. With the higher price tag of an all-inclusive cruise, the clientele are sophisticated enough to know when to stop (usually).

If cost is your primary concern, skip all-inclusive cruises.

Level of service

On small yachts there may be no service, but usually that means you help yourself. We were diving recently on a sailing charter to the Exumas that had a beer tap on deck. Serve yourself.

Even the less expensive cruise lines offer good food and service. If they don't, they lose customers. But on large ships with inexpensive cruises you will not be treated with the same attention as on the smaller and more expensive ships.

Big vs small

Big ships hide the fact that you're at sea. You will rarely feel the motion. What you will feel is the constant throng of people. You won't develop rapport with the staff and maybe not with other passengers. When you disembark in small ports your fellow passengers will overwhelm the community. On board there are activities every second of the day to keep people occupied.

The smaller the ship the more it will rock and roll with the waves. Smaller ships have fewer organized activities, but usually more than enough to keep you busy. The waiter you had yesterday will serve you today and, on the better lines, will know your preferences and your name. And, I think, you find a higher percentage of the passengers are interested in the experience and not just drinking around the pool.

Itinerary

Cruise ships are best for seeing lots of coastal places without packing your clothes every night. They provide exposure to several cities or countries without giving you great depth of substance. They can be your introduction to an area. Pick the ones you liked and go back for a more in-depth visit on your next vacation. So where do you want to go?

The itinerary sells the cruise. If you've always wanted to see the Caribbean or French Polynesia, there are dozens of itineraries. If you want to see Rome, skip the ship and fly to Rome. You won't be able to do Rome justice in the few hours of a port call. If the cruise starts or ends in Italy, then extend the visit. Many cruise lines will offer extensions or you can plan your own.

The bottom line is what lights your fire? What are you dying to see? There is probably a cruise itinerary that will cover it.

What to take?

Not much. The less the better. Your shipmates won't realize that you are wearing the same dress or shirt three times. Why bother bringing more than you really need.

You could bring a change of underwear and socks for every day.

We had two days of Semester at Sea faculty briefings before we picked up students and headed across the Pacific Ocean. Knowing I have some background in physics, one of the other faculty came to me with a problem: his electric clock. Before he plugged it in he wanted to know if it would be safe. The clock was from the U.S., so it was made for 110 volts. He had used an adapter allowing him to plug the clock into the ship's outlet which was 220 volts. I explained that it definitely would not be safe and suggested he go ashore to buy a new clock made for European outlets.

Instead he purchased a transformer to reduce the ship's voltage from 220 to 110v. He plugged his American clock into the transformer and it worked fine. But the next morning, he complained that he had overslept. The clock was slow. It had worked fine at home.

European electricity is produced at 50 Hertz or cycles per second. In the U.S., the operating frequency is 60 cycles per second. Electric clock motors move at the rate of the operating frequency. His clock was expecting 60 cycles per second, but the ship was supplying 50 cycles per second. His third try was to purchase a battery-powered clock and that worked fine.

Or, plan to wash them. Invest in travel clothing made of synthetics that dry overnight. Cotton may be comfortable, but it takes a long time to dry. Some synthetics will dry within a few hours.

Wash every night and you can get by with 3 or 4 changes of underwear and socks. Take along three or four inflatable hangers to speed up the drying. We wash in the cabin and use the laundry room once a cruise to wash bigger stuff like shirts and pants. Yes, our cabin looks like a laundry, but we don't entertain in our cabin so only our cabin steward sees it.

Dress like an onion – in layers. You don't need one jacket for every different weather condition. Pick one versatile jacket that can cover a layer for warmth when you need it.

What you really need

- **Sun glasses**
- **Hats — for sun protection, rain protection, warmth**
- **Binoculars**
- **Camera — with zoom lens**
- **Electrical adapters (see what power the ship provides)**
- **Backpack or bag to carry stuff ashore**
- **Protection for sea sickness**
- **A bag for carrying binoculars and cameras with you on the ship**

On a ship you will need to stow the luggage that carried all your stuff. Under the bed is an ideal spot, if it will fit. A cloth bag that can scrunch up is best. Large, rigid suitcases are difficult to store.

Binoculars

Binoculars or a monocular are essential to see at sea. Some of the smaller ships or yachts may provide them, but the larger ones do not. If you will purchase some optical device for your next trip at sea, check out several at a store. There is a dizzying number of models to choose from.

Look at binoculars with an optical rating of 7x32 up to 8x42. The first number refers to the magnification and the second number to the size of the objective lens. The larger the objective lens is, the more light it gathers and the better your view is. Lenses larger than 42mm makes the binoculars too heavy for most people.

Compare stabilized and not stabilized binoculars. Before I tried stabilized binoculars I didn't think they would be worth the added expense. Now I have a pair and I love them. Especially on the pitching and rolling deck of a ship, stabilization helps.

Just to muddy the water with one more consideration, after you look

Still sailing 73 years after she was built, the Astoria is a throwback to the days of ocean liners. She was considered large when built, but by today's standards she is quite small for a cruise ship. She is famous for colliding with the Andrea Doria in 1956. The Andrea Doria sank, but the Astoria, then called the Stockholm, survives and continues to provide great experiences for passengers.

at several binoculars ask to see a monocular. The advantage of having one lens is portability and light weight. They fit into a pocket or hang easily from your neck without excessive weight on your neck. A good monocular that you always have with you is better than the best binoculars that are so bulky you leave them in your stateroom.

Seasick remedies

Most people do not experience sea sickness aboard cruise ships. The ships are big, many have stabilizers to reduce rolling, and they try to avoid storms when they can. Having said that, if you're not sure if you will get sick it's better to be prepared.

It's not just the ship's motion to consider. In some ports you will have to ride a tender, a small boat, from the ship to shore. Tenders can bounce around a lot. It can take ten or fifteen minutes to load and unload at the ship and shore, all the while the tender is gyrating like a carnival ride. Ironically going ashore can be the time you most need something to ease motion sickness.

Prophylaxis can make you drowsy, which feels as bad as being sick. Make sure you get something that is non-drowsy. Try a patch. You will see some of your fellow passengers wearing one behind one ear. You can use just half a patch at first to see if that is enough.

People who wear sea bands swear they prevent sea sickness. The bands are worn around the wrist and apply pressure to a nerve.

If you know you are prone to motion sickness invest in either bands, pills, or patches. Otherwise rely on the ship's motion being slight with the fallback position of buying something at the ship's store. Also check the itinerary carefully. For each port it should state if you will be docking or "tendering."

How to pack

Into your carry-on bag go medicines you might need while waiting for your lost luggage to show up. You could also include your swimsuit so you can enjoy the day by the pool before your cabin is ready to occupy. In colder climates a warmer coat, hat, and gloves allow you to be outside while the crew is working on your room.

Rolling vs. folding? Rolling creates more dead space between each item, so it takes up more room. You can sit on your suitcase to compress everything in which case the great roll vs fold debate becomes mute. I like to lay clothing flat as much as I can to eliminate rolling. Socks, underwear, and other small stuff gets wedged in to fill spaces between shoes and other larger items. Breakable stuff gets packed among squishable stuff or inside shoes. My wife likes to have everything folded and placed inside zippered cases that

go into the suitcase. To my mind those cases are just extra weight that also reduce my options for squeezing in that last item.

We travel four to six months a year, so we do the packing thing a lot. I set out the bag days before the trip and start loading it. Each day I'll add something or take something out as I've had more time to think about what I'll really need. I check the weather report each day and think of the activities we are likely to do. Until the final zipper is zipped shut and locked, I keep changing things.

Before you head out the door for the airport, take a photo of your luggage with your smart phone. If the airline manages to send it to Timbuktu having the photo can make it easier to describe to the airline agent. Also take a photo of your passport in case that goes AWOL as well.

When to go

Cruising is a seasonal sport. Watch the pattern cruise ships make in the Atlantic: winter in the Caribbean, summer in Europe. Between the two dominant seasons are crossings (often a bargain). In season travel means rubbing shoulders with lots of others. Generally, it means good weather.

If you have choice when you travel at sea, obviously pick better weather. Winters in the North Atlantic or North Pacific can be nasty. Some

The setting sun and rising sun deliver beautiful lighting for photographs. This small freighter was sailing down the Thames River as we were headed to Greenwich.

people think it would be fun to bounce around in rough weather, but I attest it is not. A few days of bruises from running into bulkheads, not being able to walk in a straight line, and queasiness from ocean motion will convince you that calm is good.

As a general statement, September is a good month for travel. The northern hemisphere summer is over, in most places fall weather has not kicked in, and summer crowds are back at work. The big caveat is that early fall is in the heart of hurricane

season in the Northern hemisphere. Weather forecasters can alert you to tropical depressions before they become storms. Once the storm forms they can predict with some accuracy where it will go. Of course you have probably purchased your tickets weeks or longer in advance, long before they issue storm warnings. In the later summer and early fall you take your chance.

Near the equator, aside from monsoon wind changes, conditions are usually the same year-round. And at latitudes less than about 10 degrees, hurricanes rarely intrude.

To sail around South America or cruise to the Antarctic cruises run from December through February. Around Australia or New Zealand, the austral summer months are best. Winter in the northern hemisphere is summer south of the equator.

To check on weather conditions do a search for "climate graph" for port cities you want to visit. Climate graphs give you monthly averages for high and low temperatures and show precipitation.

To get current conditions and forecasts at sea, check marine forecasts. A good place to start is **Passage Weather** on the web. For a fun look at current ocean and atmospheric conditions go to **Earth NullSchool.**

A ship's tender carries people and supplies between ship and shore. It also serves as a lifeboat. Photo by Barbara Sobey.

Chapter 2

Down to the Sea in Ships

What can you see from the dock?

IT'S EXCITING TO GET THAT FIRST GLIMPSE OF THE ship that will take you on new adventures. Maybe you are returning to an old friend or about to make acquaintance with a new ship. You want to get onboard as fast as you can. But first, take a few minutes to look at the ship before you board.

Standing on the dock you see different markings on the hull. The most complex is the load line. It is located midship at the waterline. When you spot it you first notice the 30 cm (about 1 foot) circle or Load Line Disk. A solid horizontal line passes through the circle and extends

beyond the circle. The upper edge of that line is the Plimsoll line.

The Plimsoll line is aligned with the summer load line. Since sea water density depends on its temperature and salinity, it is different throughout the World Ocean and seasons. Ships ride higher in more dense water. In cold winter conditions in sea water, ships ride highest. So ships can show a series of markings off to the side for Tropical (T), Tropical fresh (TF), Fresh (F), Winter temperate (W), and Winter North Atlantic (WNA) waters.

On either side of the Load Line Disk are two letters. These are

Samuel Plimsoll was a British MP who got legislation passed to require ships to show their safe loading. Loading a ship so it sits lower in the water and has less buoyancy is dangerous and illegal. Britain was losing as many as six ships a day at sea before this legislation was passed. Plimsoll led a courageous fight to save lives of sailors.

The load line marks the legal limit to how much load a ship can carry. BV indicates that the certificating agency is Bureau Veritas, a French company. The letters AB is for the American Bureau of Shipping and LR is for Lloyd's Registry. There are a half dozen other agencies. Ships that carry passengers and cargo, as this ship does, can have alternative certificate levels depending on how much space is for passengers and how much is for cargo. The P1 level is for passengers. The F is the load line for fresh water. Since fresh water is less dense than salt water, the ship will sit lower in the fresh water.

Just behind the bow is the symbol for the bulbous bow to warn smaller boaters to avoid this area. Behind this will be symbols for one or multiple bow thrusters. Similar markings for stern thrusters are just in front of the stern.

abbreviations for the company that certified the ship's load line. LR is for Lloyds Register and AB is for American Bureau of Shipping. There are several other companies that register ships.

Most ships today have a bulbous bow. You can see it while the ship is tied up in port. The prow or cut-water of the ship curves backward from its forward-most projection towards the water line. Below the water surface

The bulbous bow projects forward of the prow or cutwater. It reduces drag on the ship so it improves speed and reduces fuel consumption. On the port side is the symbol for the bulbous bow to warn small boats to avoid running into it. Wrapped around the bulb is an oil boom to contain any oil spilled during refueling on the port side.

This ship is riding so high you can see the bow thruster just above the water, aft of the anchor chain.

Thrusters allow ships to maneuver sideways. The electric motor propeller can push water to either side. Here the wake of the propeller is visible. In shallow water thrusters kick up plumes of sediment visible from the deck.

the hull protrudes forward in a cylindrical shape. This odd-looking extension reduces drag, making the propulsion more efficient, and saving fuel. To warn boaters to stay away from this underwater extension of the ship in port, the crew will hang a rope with a flag over the bulbous bow. And, on the side of the ship you will see a symbol showing the outline of the bow and the bulb. This symbol is an additional warning for small boats to avoid hitting the bulbous bow.

Most cruise ships today have thrusters to help them maneuver in and out of port. The thrusters are

electric motors with propellers that can push water to either side. They are mounted into the hull. You can see them clearly on ships in dry dock. To warn boaters to stay away, the locations of the thrusters are indicated with the symbol of a propeller inside a circle. There will be one symbol for each thruster, and the bigger the ship, the more thrusters it will have. They can also have thrusters near the stern, too.

Many cruise ships have stabilizers. These are underwater wings or fins that reduce the rolling of the ship. To deploy, the thrusters rotate outward from the hull. In position they look like wings on an airplane, underwater. They rotate to provide upward lift

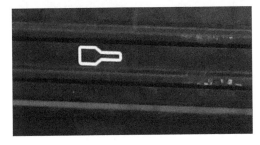

Although you can't see a ship's stabilizer while it is in port, you can see its location. This symbol warns tugs and boats to avoid this area.

The mooring lines could be highways for rats to climb aboard. To keep them in port and not on the ship rat guards are lashed onto the lines.

Lines are secured on bollards bolted to the dock.

rat guard on it. The rat guards are light-weight metal plates tied onto the lines to keep vermin from joining the cruise.

The lines are secured to a bollard. These are heavy duty steal fixtures bolted to the dock.

If the ship or boat is taking on fuel, the port may require an oil boom to surround it. This floating structure keeps any spilled oil from escaping, making it easier to clean up.

The ship moves up, then moves down: Tides

One thing you will notice in port is the effect of tides. Over a few hours ships at dock rise and fall. In some ports they will rise a lot and in others you will barely notice a change. Also in port you might be able to see where tides and sea level are measured.

An oil boom is being rigged around the ship before fueling begins.

on the side that is rolling downward and downward lift on the side that is rolling upward. Thus they counteract the rolling motion. The stabilizers are too far beneath the surface to see, but you will see the warning symbol on the side of the ship. The symbol is the outline of two rectangles that have been smashed together.

Notice the several heavy lines or hawsers holding the ship to the dock. Ropes on a ship become lines when they are used for a specific purpose. Hawsers are ropes that are at least as big around as your hand. Each of the lines (hawsers) holding the ship has a name. Spring lines stop the ship or boat from moving parallel to the dock, so they angle ahead or behind the ship. The bow line and stern line secure the ship so it doesn't move away from the dock. Each line has a

Tides are caused by the gravitational attraction principally by the moon, secondarily the sun, and to a lesser degree the planets. As the earth revolves around the sun it also rotates on its axis, in essence rotating in front of the moon and sun. The exact path of this motion is the result of gravitational attraction of astronomical bodies. The surface water is also attracted by these gravitational forces and, being liquid, behaves differently than the solid earth.

The moon has more influence over tides than does the sun even though it is so much smaller than the sun. The sun has a mass 27 million times larger than the moon's. However the distance between the moon and earth is 238,900 miles vs. the distance from earth to sun of approximately 93 million miles. In the equation for gravitation attraction, distance dominates over mass so the sun is about half as strong as the moon in generating tides.

If the planet were completed covered by deep water, high tide would always occur beneath the moon. As the moon revolves around the earth, the high tide would follow

it. But the oceans aren't deep enough to allow the tidal wave to keep up with the rotation of the earth. Waves, and the tide is a wave, travel slower in shallow water. And, someone dropped all those continents into the ocean making it impossible for the tidal wave to travel around the planet.

When a ship is loading hazardous or flammable cargo, it flies the "Bravo" flag. Bravo is the name given to the flag for the letter B. The ship was loading fuel in Iceland, so that country's flag is also flown.

So instead of simply residing underneath the moon, tides are complex. In the middle of the ocean the difference in height of the sea surface due to tides is at most a foot and a half. Only in geographies where there is a funneling of water do tides get large. And, if the bay has a natural frequency of 12 hours, the tides resonate. They can get huge.

Hold a weight on a string. With even the mildest hand motion at exactly the right rate, you can get the weight to gyrate wildly. That precise rate is the natural frequency of the pendulum. Bays act the same way. The Bay of Fundy is finely tuned to the tidal cycle and its tidal range can be 50'.

Such huge tidal ranges don't occur every day. Only when the earth, moon, and sun are aligned so the gravitation attraction is maximum do large tides happen. When not aligned the sun's gravity and the moon's gravity operate perpendicular to each other, preventing a large attraction. Alignment is called "syzygy" and "spring" tides occur then. "Neap" tides are the opposite condition when the tidal range is a minimum.

Tidal stations

Around the world there are thousands of stations that measure and record the height of the sea surface. These are tide stations. In the U.S. you can find the data on line and you can find predictions for almost anywhere in the world. Look up NOAA (National Oceanic and Atmospheric Administration) tide tables.

Look around the ship while it is in port to see a tide gauging station. Often it is in a small or tiny shack at the end of a pier. Sometimes the station is an exposed pipe with a box on top. In either case a pipe goes out the bottom of the shed or box straight down into the water. At the roof of the shed or box is a high frequency UHF antenna.

Near the bottom of the pipe beyond your vision are a series of

Tide measuring stations are in most ports around the world. Some are as inconspicuous as this one. The instrumentation and radio to transmit the data are located on top of a pipe that is attached to the dock.

holes that let water in and out. The level of water inside the pipe is measured either mechanically (with a float) or electronically (bouncing a signal off the surface and timing its return). A recording device and a radio transmitter are housed either in a box you can see or inside the shack.

More obvious will be the ship's vertical movement alongside the dock. You can notice the angle the brow or gangway changes throughout the day. Sometimes the crew will change the disembarkation deck as the ship moves higher or lower.

Find your way aboard

It helps to speak the local language, even on a ship where everyone speaks English. So, here are a few vocabulary words.

Port side is on the left, when facing the bow or pointy end. Starboard is on the right when facing forward. Stern is the rear end of the ship. Midship is halfway in between.

Port is left because before steering wheels, ships tied up to docks so the left-side was facing the dock. So dockside was port side. Why, you may ask, did ships tie up on the left side? Because most steersmen were right handed. So, the tiller, the bar that attached to the rudder allowing a steersman to steer, was on the right side. To protect the tiller from being damaged as the ship moved at the dock, it was always kept opposite the dock. Starboard comes from the Old English word meaning the side the ship is steered from. All of this so you can find your cabin when you know it's on port or starboard.

Even numbered staterooms will be on the port side (usually) and odd on the starboard. Theaters are usually forward on one of the lower decks. Dining is usually aft. The more formal dining areas are on lower decks, probably on the deck with the purser's desk or reception. Usually a less formal dining area serving cafeteria style will be on one of the top decks, all the way aft. The gangway or opening leading to the gangplank or brow will be on one of the lower levels. In port the ship will use different gangways on different decks depending on the height of the dock and the range of tides.

By the way, you will be on a ship or a boat. The two terms do not mean the same thing. On cruise ships it's common to hear passengers call it a boat, but it's a ship! What's the difference? A boat can be picked up and carried aboard a ship. A ship cannot be picked up. You could quibble that a floating dry dock can pick up a ship turning it into a boat, but we won't quibble. Of course if your vessel is small you're on a boat and the experience will be very different.

Best viewing locations

Generally the top weather deck offers the best ocean viewing. With 360 degree viewing, the ability to scoot from port to starboard quickly, and for the most distant visibility possible this is the place to be. However, as you walk around the ship take note of alternative spots.

When the ship is heading directly into the wind standing on the top weather deck can be uncomfortable. With the ship moving at maybe 20 knots coupled with a 20-knot head wind, 40 knots of wind power are in your face. The upper decks often have partitions you can stand behind to get some lee, but if they don't shield you go elsewhere.

Try the promenade deck. This deck is lower and provides some shelter from the wind. You can't see as far into the ocean from this lower deck, but in rough seas you can't see much of anything anyway. If it's raining this makes this covered deck an even better option - you won't feel like you're being given a power washing.

Farther to the aft you can find other protected areas. At the stern you can find a sweet spot with very little wind when the ship is heading into the wind. Another advantage here is that some pelagic birds tend to follow ships and boats and this is the place to see them.

In general, you don't want to be squinting into the sun. Visibility is better as is your comfort when viewing with the sun at your back.

If you want to avoid as much of the ship motion as possible, be midship on the lowest weather deck (deck exposed to the weather). Standing here you can see how far the bow and stern rise and fall with each passing wave. The vertical motion can be impressive.

How far can I see?

The higher you are on the ship, the farther you can see. Weather permitting, of course. Standing on the upper deck of your ship, how far can you see? The quick answer is about 12 miles. If you know the height of the deck above the sea surface you can get a more accurate answer.

How much of a geek are you? If the answer is full tilt, try this. Count the number of steps from the water line to the upper deck. Step height is about 7.5", but pull out your travel ruler to confirm that.

Counting steps is necessary as the height of each deck can be different. Decks with passenger cabins are typically about 9.6'. Decks with public spaces are significantly taller, 14' to 16'. Counting the steps gives a better estimate than just counting the number of decks and multiplying by an assumed average deck height.

To get the height from the water line to the first deck, you'll have to wait until you do a tender landing. As you walk down to the tender count the steps until your foot hits the tender deck. Your feet will be close to sea level.

Easier is to find the height of decks on a ship's plan. If you don't find this in the passageways, ask the deck officer during a bridge tour.

With your estimate of the height of the deck above the surface of the sea, add the height of your eyeballs. That extra 5 or 6 feet makes a difference. Say the height of your eyeballs is 100' above the surface. Take the square root of that height, 10, and multiply that by 1.3 to get distance in miles to the horizon. In this case, 13 miles.

Spinning your eyeballs 360 degrees avails them of the sight of some 82 square miles of the ocean. That's a lot of water! But it's only 0.00006% of the ocean's surface area.

Of course weather plays a dominant role in how far you can see. Fog can cut visibility to a few meters. But assuming the skies are clear and unobstructed, the limitation is your height and the height of what you are looking at.

It's common to see the top of a ship above the horizon when the ship's hull is below the horizon. Curvature of the earth limits how far we can see horizontally. Looking straight up you can see millions of miles to distant stars. Horizontally not so far.

Chapter 3

Getting Underway and Tying Up

Before sailing

STANDING ON THE UPPER DECK YOU WATCH AS the last passengers come aboard. The crew starts to dismantle the gangway, taking off the safety net and removing the vinyl side panels. When everyone is on-board, the brow or gangway is lifted onto the ship. In some ports the port authority may provide the brow that is removed by crane or fork lift.

Activity rises on the bridge wings – those structures that protrude outward from the bridge. Here the captain, first officer, deck officer, and pilot will be gathered. Typically the pilot will observe and comment as needed. The captain will operate the bow and stern thrusters and will give commands to the quartermaster at the helm inside the bridge. The first officer will direct the line handlers and will receive reports from the

other officers who are stationed at the bow and stern.

Particulates in ship's exhaust gases become condensate nuclei that form clouds from water vapor. As ships move they leave behind a line of clouds that can be seen from space. NASA satellite photographs of the ocean can show these tracks

The pilot, ship's captain and first officer control the ship from the port wing. Standing on this lateral extension of the bridge the officers have a better view of the line handling and of the ship's position relative to the dock.

Satellites can detect the passage of ships from their exhaust gases. Photo by NOAA.

When the pilot steps aboard the "Hotel" flag is raised. It is lowered as soon as he steps ashore (coming into port) or steps onto a pilot boat (leaving port). "Hotel" is the flag for the letter "h."

The ship's diesel engines will start well before departing. In port the ship will operate one diesel engine to turn the generator to provide electrical power. Some ships will rely on "shore power" but most will generate their own. As sailing time approaches other diesel engines are started and you can feel the vibrations throughout the ship. Standing on the deck you might notice the dark exhaust coming from the stack.

The pilot

If the pilot is aboard, the pilot flag will be flying. In the alphabet of nautical flags it is the "H" or "hotel" flag. It is a square flag, divided in the middle vertically. Red on one side and white on the other. When the pilot leaves the ship and steps down to the pilot boat so he can return to port, the pilot flag is lowered.

Watch the pilot leaving the ship. With calm seas he nimbly steps off the ship and onto the pilot boat waiting alongside. To accommodate the transfer the ship slows and holds a steady course and the pilot boat comes up from behind the ship.

In rough seas the pilot boat bounces up and down while the much larger ship does not. The pilot has to time his transfer carefully to minimize the gap between the two. Usually the pilot boat has crew to assist or catch him.

Coming into port the pilot transfer is also fun to watch. You'll see the boat approach, circle behind

When a pilot is onboard who is in charge, the captain or pilot? The captain always has ultimate responsibility for the ship. In normal circumstances the pilot advises the captain in the form of direct orders to the helmsmen. The captain can overrule the pilot. However, in the Panama Canal the pilot is responsible for the ship's navigation.

In busy ports ships contribute a lot of air pollution to the city atmosphere. Undoubtedly some cities will try to reduce this pollution in the future and ships will have to add scrubbers to their smoke stacks to remove the combustion particles and gases or find other ways to reduce them.

Line handlers on the dock grab the monkey's fist on the end of the throwing line and haul in the line that is tied to a heavier mooring line.

Pilots ride out to ships coming into ports on pilot boats. The pilot boat will circle behind the ship and come forward while the ship slows down.

All the mooring lines will be doubled up. A second line is added for each mooring position. Here a boat was used to secure the stern line and now to double up. With no dock space available, the ship is anchored at the bow and the stern is secured to this mooring point.

the ship, and come up on the far side so it is adjacent to a door in the side of the ship. On older ships the pilot might have to climb a rope ladder to board, but not on cruise ships.

Lines

Ships and ropes go together. More so on a sailing vessel, but even cruise ships rely on miles of rope. When the twisted fiber or steel comes out of the factory it is rope. When it has an assigned duty, it becomes a line. A rope used to secure the bow to a mooring becomes a line, specifically the bowline. When that line is so big that your fingers cannot reach around it, it is a hawser.

One special line is the throwing line. As a ship approaches a dock a sailor will heave a throwing line to line handlers ashore. The line will have a "monkey's fist" knot at its end to give it weight so it carries farther. The line handlers grab the throwing line and pull it in. The end of the throwing line is tied to the much heavier lines or hawsers they will loop around a bollard on the dock.

When all the lines have been secured, the process will be repeated with second lines to "double up."

Watch how the line handlers secure the second lines. They don't just loop them over the bollards on top of the first line. They thread the eye of the second line up through the eye of the first line and then loop it over the bollard. This way they can later release either line without having to slack both lines.

A seaman tosses the throwing line to workers on the dock. The throwing line is light, so it can be thrown far. It is tied to a heavier mooring line that the dock workers secure to a bollard. Then the ship's winches are used to pull in the slack and secure the ship to the dock.

All the mooring lines have names. The bowline and stern line hold the ship to the dock. They are perpendicular to the ship and dock. A similar line in the middle of the ship is called the breast line.

Spring lines prevent the ship from sliding forward or backward along the dock. There are two pairs of these: one pair is near the bow of the ship and the other is near the stern of the ship. The pair near the front are called forward bow spring (this one angles forward from the ship) and the after bow spring line (this angles backward

or toward the stern). The other pair are the forward quarter spring line and the after quarter spring line. The lines are checked periodically and moved as the tide changes.

In departing the process is reversed. Before the port line handlers arrive notice that the lines are "doubled up." Instead of having one line or hawser holding the ship at each position, there are two. As sailing approaches the line handlers show up, the crew on board release tension on one member of each pair of lines, and the shore crew pull those doubled lines off the bollards on the dock. The ship's crew winches the heavy lines back on board. The ship will be left with one set of lines securing it to the dock until the final cast off command is given.

Bow and stern thrusters

When all is ready the ship's crew will release tension on these lines one by one. One line might be held fast until the thrusters at the opposite end of the ship swing the ship away from the dock. The bow and stern thrusters allow the officers to pull the ship sideways away from the dock without employing (and paying for) a tug. Strong winds pushing the ship onto the dock may require a tug to give assistance. But tugs are expensive so the captain will be reluctant to employ one unless it is really necessary.

Next time you're in port look for the symbols indicating the location of thrusters. It is a circle with four parts suggesting a propeller. These are a few feet above the water line. Large cruise ships may have three bow thrusters and one or two stern thrusters.

The thrusters are electric motors with propeller blades mounted into the hull of the ship. You will hear and feel the vibrations when they operate. You can also see the sediments they kick up as a dirty cloud in the water.

Ship's horn

Cover your ears as the ship's horn is about to blast. One long blast announces "I am underway." Three blasts signals "I am operating in reverse." The other signal you sometimes hear on leaving and entering port is 5 or more short blasts that tells another ship that they need to do something to avoid collision. Quite often a weekend sailor or lazy ship's captain will get in the way of a much larger ship.

At sea seven short blasts followed by a long blast sends you to your emergency station. Your station is indicated both on a placard on the inside of your cabin door and on your life preserver. The preservers are stowed usually inside the clothes closet, but can also be found underneath the bed. Make sure you are familiar with what to do in case of an emergency.

As the ship pulls out of the harbor the public address starts blaring their favorite departure song. If you're lucky, waiters are wandering the decks offering glasses of champagne. Bon voyage!

Tying up

Coming into port reverses the sequence of events of leaving. The pilot boat brings the pilot out to the ship. A crew member will hoist the pilot flag and the quarantine flag. The quarantine flag indicates that the ship has not been cleared to enter the port and is requesting permission to do so. In the middle ages a ship might have to wait in the harbor for 40 days before permission was given to come ashore. This delay ensured that any infectious diseases would manifest themselves. The word quarantine is derived from the Venetian word for 40. A ship under quarantine will fly the flag for the letter L, Lima.

The quarantine flag, solid yellow, is raised when entering a port. The flag shows that the ship is requesting a pratique or permission to enter the port. Also note in this picture that the Norwegian flag is flying as the ship is coming into a Norwegian port.

With the advice of the pilot, the captain will bring the ship to the dock. A crew member will toss the heaving line to line handlers on the dock and the ship will be tied up. Lines will be doubled and rat guards will be set.

Chapter 4

Whales, Dolphins, Turtles, Birds, Flying Fish, and More

The depressing numbers

THE GOOD NEWS IS THAT THERE ARE MILLIONS of animals patiently waiting for you to step onto the deck and start looking. And, with persistence and a bit of luck you will see them.

The bad news is that it will take persistence and luck. In general, populations of large marine animals are down 90% from 50 - 100 years ago. That provocative statistic should disturb you.

Certainly not all species populations are down that far, and some are not down at all. Several species of whales have rebounded nicely from population lows in 1966 when most whaling ended. Gray whale populations along the U.S., Canada, and Mexican west coast now exceed what we think were historic levels. On the other hand, there are only a few hundred right whales living and they could become extinct in the next few years.

The population declines are not just among marine mammals. Shark populations are down 90% and so are pelagic bird populations. Some populations of sea lions have been reduce by 94%.

Coral reefs with their high diversity of animals have been decimated by bleaching events. High ocean temperatures, increased ocean acidity, and disease have reduced healthy reefs by at least 50%.

The grasses of the ocean are microscopic marine plants, called phytoplankton. These plants convert sunlight into carbohydrates through photosynthesis and are consumed by tiny animals, zooplankton, and larger animals that capture the plants by filtering them out of seawater.

Corals ingest, but do not digest, some of the phytoplankton. Living inside the coral animal, these plants continue to convert sunlight into food. They produce up to nine times more food than they need and this excess feeds the corals. This arrangement benefits both the plants and coral. The plants get a safe place to live and the coral gets free food – a symbiotic relationship.

But when water temperatures rise too high, the corals expel the plants. In the process of photosynthesis the plants produce oxygen and with higher temperatures the increased oxygen becomes toxic to the corals, so they eject the plants.

When you are diving on a coral reef you can see bleached coral. You may also notice some corals look almost normal but have a white or black ring around part. These corals are infected with a disease.

Global warming stresses the corals and makes them more susceptible to disease. The increased carbon dioxide in the atmosphere also increases the acidity of ocean waters. In recent years the oceans have become 30% more acidic and this higher level of acidity erodes shells of animals. Higher temperatures, increased acidity, and disease are destroying the coral reefs.

This coral has a disease, probably caused by stress induced by climate change. This is on the Belize reef, second largest coral reef system.

Not just coral reefs, sharks, and whales have suffered. Fish populations have been decimated. The numbers of large fish have declined dramatically and some fish species have been hunted to near extinction.

Most of the great fisheries that fed the world 50 years ago have crashed or are in danger of crashing. Not all have crashed; a few are well-managed. But the crash of the Canadian Atlantic Cod fishery and the Peruvian Anchovy fishery should have scared us into action. They didn't. We harvest fewer wild fish today than we did in 2000 and projections are that the decline will continue for decades. An ecological crash in the ocean is occurring. On your cruise you will see it and hear it.

You will hear it when people say, "I thought there would be more birds out here." "I thought we'd see lots of whales." You will notice it in what you don't see: lots of marine life. There are still millions of amazing animals to see, but only a tiny fraction of what you could have seen a few decades ago.

I apologize for starting this chapter on wildlife in such a negative tone. But the oceans are sick and the political leadership needed to heal them is absent. If you love being at sea and seeing what is left of the wildlife, please support any of the dozens of environmental groups that are fighting to protect and restore the seas.

In the meantime, cherish every view of whales, turtles, dolphins, and pelagic birds. The generations that follow you may not have the opportunity.

Whales

Whales come in two varieties: those with teeth and those without. The ones without teeth have baleen plates and are called baleen whales. The baleen plates are giant sieves that the whales use to filter food from the water. The plates are composed of material similar to your fingernails.

There are 17 species of baleen whales and more than 70 species of toothed whales including dolphins.

A humpback blows along the coast of Mexico. The blow is mostly condensed water vapor in the air expelled by the whale. The blow of a humpback whale is in the shape of a mushroom.

Experts quibble over the number of species and quite a few species are rarely seen. We'll stick to the ones you're most likely to see.

Whales with baleen plates have two blowholes on the top of their head. If you look closely you can see two streams of water and condensation arising from the twin holes. But you have to look closely as the two streams merge and appear to be one. Only the right whales have two distinct streams. Toothed whales, on the other hand, have one blowhole.

In either case, the spout is mostly condensed air. As whales exhale they force out warm, moist air from their lungs into the cooler and lower pressure atmosphere. Instant condensation occurs. There is also some water from around the blowhole that gets caught in the stream, but most of the blow is condensed air from the whales' lungs.

Whales with baleen plates either have throat pleats or not. Blue, Humpback, Fin, Sei, and Minke whales all have throat pleats. If a whale exposes its underside to you in a breach, you will see the pleats. There can be as many as 100 pleats. These allow the throat to expand to hold a giant mouthful of water and food. Then these "rorqual" whales push the water out of their mouths with their tongues that weight hundreds of pounds. The water passes through the comb-like baleen plates and back into the ocean. Small fish and shrimp that were caught in the mouthful of seawater are trapped on the inside of the baleen plates. The giant tongue licks the inside of the plates so the goodies can be swallowed. When the mouth is not full of water and food, the pleats fold together to reduce the drag as the whale swims.

Some whales have baleen plates and are not rorquals. That is they filter feed, but don't have pleats in their throats. Gray whales feed on the bottom. Right whales have huge, oversized mouths with very long baleen plates. If you see a piece of baleen in a museum that is longer than 6', it's from a right or bowhead whale.

Breaching, spy hops, and fin slaps

If King Neptune is smiling on you, you may see the whale breach, spy hop, or do a tail or fin slap. A breach is a whale coming out of the water head first. Humpback whales swim up to 18 miles per hour parallel to the surface and then angle upwards

and out of the water. Other species, like sperm whales, come up vertically, rise out of the water, and crash back down.

This breaching humpback whale exposes its throat pleats. The pleats extend from its jaw all the way to its stomach. They allow the throat to expand like an accordion so the whale can gulp a huge amount of water and food. Photo by Sally Mizrock.

The breaching whale's return to the water is a spectacular splash as tons of water are sprayed into the air. This is one of the greatest views in nature. Picture an animal the size of a school bus shooting out of the water and doing a belly flop. Totally grand.

The twin blowholes of a baleen whale are easy to see on this Fin whale. All baleen whales have two blowholes, but two spouts can be seen only coming from right whales. Photo by Sally Mizrock.

A whale holds its tail up, out of the water. We call this behavior "tail sailing" but we doubt that the whale is using wind power to move. Photo by Will Hayes.

Whales will also raise one pectoral fin out of the water and slap it on the surface. They will do it over and over again. Some will hold a vertical position in the water with their head down and slap their fluke over and over. This is lob tailing. We watched one do a dozen tail slaps in a row, while holding its breathe. We don't know what this behavior means, but some have suggested it could be a way to make sound or it could be a sign of aggression. Aggression, as get away from me.

Others will hold their bodies vertically and raise their heads out of the water. Gray whales and humpback whales do this "spy hopping." It

The motion of a whale's tail makes an ephemeral print on the water surface that you can see on calm days.

appears that they are trying to get a better look at us.

One more whale behavior to look for is "tail sailing." Here a whale will hold a position of head down and tail up and out of the water. It looks as if the whale is trying to get the breeze on its tail.

If the winds are light and the water surface calm, you may see "fluke prints" on the surface. These are the trail of whales, made by the motion of the tail. Native hunters apparently could detect whales by seeing their fluke prints.

When you see a spout or a splash here are a few things to look for so you can identify the whale. What does the spout look like? Most whales' spouts rise vertically. Of course a brisk wind will quickly blow the spout downwind, but you can tell if it's vertically initially. If instead the blow angles forward at a 45 degree angle, you are lucky enough to be looking at sperm whales.

Sailing northward along the Natal Coast of South Africa one afternoon we passed twenty or thirty pods of humpback whales on their way south. Each pod had three to five whales. They were headed to their summer feeding grounds in Antarctica and they were excited to be on their way. They had not eaten for a month, and they were looking forward to a seafood banquet. For three or four hours I stood on the deck of the Semester at Sea's Explorer watching the humpbacks breach. It was spectacular afternoon.

If the blow is bi-furcated or split into two streams, you're looking at the much endangered right whale. There are several species of right whales, but their blow is always bi-furcated. In the Arctic, bowhead whales also have a bi-furcated spout.

All other whales spout vertically. The blue whale exhales a giant spout, up to 25 or 30' above the ocean surface. The fin and Sei whales have somewhat shorter spouts. Humpbacks' spout is mushroom shaped. The spouts of smaller dolphins are difficult to see.

Gray whales

Gray whales make the longest migration of any mammal. Annually they travel from the Arctic Seas around Alaska down to Mexico. Their population is higher now than it has

A gray whale dives off the coast of Alaska. Grays are alone among the great whales as the one species that feeds on the sea floor. Photo by Rob Avery.

ever been. These whales are poster children for marine conservation.

If you cruise up the Inside Passage in summer to Alaska, you will see gray whales. Although many swim past Southeast Alaska and continue

up into the Bering, Chukchi, and Beaufort Seas, some stop along the way and spend their summers in Southeast Alaska.

The annual migration northward begins in February or March. By April many of the whales will have arrived in Southeast Alaska. In the early fall they head south arriving in Mexico at the end of fall or early winter. You can see them migrating along the coasts of Washington, Oregon, and California. At some coastal towns you can see them from shore.

Unlike other baleen whales, grays feed on the bottom. They take three or four breaths and then dive for 5 to 10 minutes. They plow the bottom with their mouths open. They bulldoze the bottom, always using the right side of their mouths to pick up worms, clams, and lots of sand. Their tongues push their mouthful of water and good stuff to eat outward, trapping the good stuff to eat in their baleen plates. With a lick of their tongue they wipe clean their baleen, and then swallow their snack. Constantly worn down by the sand, their baleen plates are quite short.

Since they feed on the bottom they stay in shallow water. Hence you may be able to see them from shore in their migration as they hug the coast.

At sea or ashore you're most likely to notice their spout: 5' or higher.

Two humpback whales spy hop or appear to be looking at the photographer.

With 26,000 whales confined to the coast areas, you'll bound to see them. Timing is critical. They travel south in the fall and north in the summer. You can also see them in the lagoons of Baja, Mexico in winter as well as in coastal Alaska in summer.

Humpback whales

Everyone's favorite, humpback whales seem to be doing well. Their population is growing. Like grays, humpbacks migrate seasonally. They travel poleward in summer to feast on the rich bounty of krill (shrimp) or fish. In winter they migrate to warmer waters to mate and give birth. Alaska in summer and Hawaii in winter are great spots to see these magnificent animals.

You can identify humpback whales by their blow. It has a mushroom shape as at the top the blow falls outward and downward. Their pectoral (side) fins are huge, much larger than the fins of other whales.

The leading edge of each fin is lined with bumps.

These help cut hydrodynamic drag on the fins. Like other whales humpbacks will take several breathes at the surface before diving deep. In diving the humpback earns its name as it arches its back sharply just as its dorsal fin arises from the sea. Then it lifts its flukes to help push it down.

Two humpbacks arrive at the surface with mouths wide open, full of food and water. Photo by NOAA.

Southern hemisphere humpbacks feed on the abundant krill in the water off Antarctica. Northern hemisphere humpbacks feed mainly on schools of fish that they hunt cooperatively with other members of their pod.

A humpback whale in Alaska blows before it dives. Photo by Rob Avery.

A pod of humpback comes to the surface feeding in the Drake Passage. Photo by Charles Ford.

As far as we know the northern and southern populations don't mix and don't cross the equator.

If you're very lucky you might see a pod of humpbacks hunting cooperatively, using a bubble net. One whale swims beneath a school of small fish and blows bubbles to surround the fish and herd them into a concentrated cylinder. The other members of the pod swim upward through the dense school with mouths wide open. If you're close enough you can see the circle of bubbles on the surface and then two or three whales breaking the surface with their mouths full. Their normally streamlined throats will be stretched out, the expansion allowed by the pleats.

Sounds in the sea can travel incredible distances. Sea water is about 780 times denser than air. This allows sound to travel four times faster in water with little loss of energy. The ocean also has a sound channel that concentrates sounds allowing them to be heard far away. The "silent sea" isn't silent at all.

Humpbacks are the singing whales. Males sing extraordinary songs that can be heard across oceans. Other males pick up a tune they hear, modify it and incorporate it into their musical arrangements.

Not only do they sing, they dance. These are the whales that perform out-of-water acrobatics that are, I claim, the greatest show in the animal kingdom.

And one more interesting tidbit from a recent observation. It appears that humpbacks interrupt orca trying to kill other whales. Orca will go after baby gray whales by separating the baby from its mother and drowning it. As the baby tries to surface to grab a breath, the orcas will swim on top of it, pushing it down. Unable to breathe, the baby quickly tires and drowns providing a rich meal for the orca. Recently a pod of humpbacks was seen intervening in an orca hunt and apparently thwarting it. Does this happen often? Why would one whale species come to the aid of a different whale species? There's so much we don't know.

Blue whales

Bigger than the biggest dinosaur, blue whales can be nearly 100' long. You're unlikely to see any that approach that length, but they are still the biggest animals on earth.

At sea you will notice the blue-gray color of the back of the whale as it comes up to blow. The blow is tall and narrow, typically 30' high but can be higher. The fin on its back is comically small and located close to the tail. And you will notice that it is big; bigger than other whales you've seen. If lucky enough to see one, you will probably see only one. They usually travel by themselves unless you see a mother together with her calf.

As the biggest animals blue whales hold a lot of first place trophies. They have the largest tongues (3 tons), largest mouths (holding almost 100 tons of water and food), largest hearts (400 pounds), and males have the longest penises (8 – 10'). If the last statistic catches your attention consider the gymnastic skills two whales must have in order to breathe and pro-create.

Blue whales are not the fastest whales. That speed title goes to the slightly smaller fin whales. But blues can push 30 miles per hour for brief periods and sustain 12 miles per hour. What would it feel like to be in the water with a 50 – 60-ton animal coming at you at 30 miles per hour? At the least it would be an impressive sight.

Like humpbacks blue whales vocalize or make sounds underwater. They are the loudest animals in the world, possibly communicating with friends or relatives thousands of miles apart.

There aren't so many blue whales. They were hunted almost to extinction. A worldwide ban was enacted in 1966 to stop hunting whales, but Russians continued to hunt them for a few years. Estimates are difficult to make and the best guess is that the population has doubled or tripled since the ban was initiated. The population today is estimated to be 1% of the natural population. Or, we can say that the population has been reduced 99%.

Right whales

Sail into Cape Town and you might be lucky enough to see the spouts or even breaching of (southern) right whales. You can also see them (northern right whales) off the coast of New England in summer. Argentina declared them a National Natural Monument. There are only a few hundred right whales in the North Atlantic and possibly 100 in the North Pacific Ocean. Fewer than two thousand southern right whales live in the Southern Hemisphere. Right whales are the most endangered of the great whales and are very close to extinction. However, the southern right whale population is growing. Although no longer hunted by man, they are killed by collisions with ships and getting entangled in fishing nets.

The most distinctive feature of right whales is their bifurcated spout. All baleen whales have two blow holes, but only right whales show separate spouts from them. If you see two distinct spouts from one whale, it is a right whale.

If you are close enough to right whales you can see callosities or roughened skin on their heads and can see their puny pectoral fins. The pectoral fins are as ridiculously small as the humpbacks' are large. Right whales don't have a dorsal fin on their back. They can grow to about 50' in length and can live to 100 years. Females are larger than males.

A right whale breaches. Notice the tiny pectoral fins and the huge mouth. Photo by NOAA

Right whales were a whaler's first choice. They carry about 40% of their body weight as fat which was profit for the whalers. The high fat content also means these whales float when they die so a whaler is more likely to keep the catch he shot and not lose it as the whale sinks.

I provided some superlative statistics for blue whales. Here is one for the right whales. The male testes are the largest in the animal kingdom. They vastly outweigh those of the blue what by a factor of 10:1. Can you believe 2,000 pounds for a pair!

If you see one or two right whales count yourself very lucky. Your children might never have the opportunity.

Orca

Orcas are toothed whales. They are included in the family of dolphins of which there are many species. Way too many to list here.

Orca are easy to identify. Their head and shoulders are black. Behind the eye is a patch of white. The undersides are white. Behind the dorsal fin is a saddle of gray. Males have tall, rigid and rectangular dorsal fins. Up to 6' tall. Female dorsal fins are smaller and curve backwards.

A male orca swims in the Drake Passage between South American and Antarctica. Photo by Charles Ford.

There are three types of orcas. Some are permanent residents of an area. These tend to be fish eaters. The best example is in the Salish Sea (Puget Sound). Transient orcas travel in small groups or pods, don't interact with resident orcas, and eat marine mammals. They tend to show up when seals, sea lions, and other marine mammals are pupping. There appears to be a third type that live offshore. These eat fish and probably marine mammals as well.

The male orca has a very tall, triangular dorsal fin. Photo by Rob Avery.

Orca are fascinating animals. Yes, they do kill whales, but attacking something much bigger than yourself is a dangerous business. One good swipe from the tail of a fin whale would produce a serious injury to an

A female orca has a curved dorsal fin that is smaller than an adult male's. Photo by Rob Avery.

A pod of long-finned pilot whales seen off the east coast of Iceland.

attacking Orca. In general orca will not attack healthy full-grown whales, but will attack babies or sick whales.

Very recently great white sharks have washed ashore with their livers removed. Some scientists think orcas are responsible. There is a wealth of videos on the web as well as text and photos to explore.

Blackfish

Orcas are part of a group of toothed whales known as blackfish. Orcas are the largest members of the group. Somewhat smaller are pilot whales (long-finned and short-

What happens to a whale when it dies? Whatever part of the carcass that isn't eaten right away near the surface will fall to the ocean bottom, becoming a "whale fall." There it will feed a host of animals, some of which live only on fallen whale carcasses. Estimates are that there could be nearly 700,000 carcasses of the largest whale species on the ocean bottom at any time. On average the carcasses are spaced about every 7 – 8 miles on the ocean floor. It takes months for the flesh to be eaten and years for the bones to be consumed.

finned), false killer whales, pygmy killer whales, and melon-headed whales.

These several species are only occasionally seen. When seen they can be in large groups. Unlike dolphins, they tend not to approach ships. But some pods will.

They don't have the distinctive color patterns of the orca. Their heads are blunt and their bodies are shorter than orca.

Not much is known about these other members of the blackfish group. Most are widely distributed throughout the ocean even if we don't see them often. Hawaii is one place to see both false killer whales and pygmy killer whales. Melon-headed whales are often seen entering and leaving Nuka Hiva in the South Pacific.

Most are thought to eat squid and fish from the depths of the ocean. Some interact with smaller dolphins and one false killer whale successfully mated with a bottle-nose dolphin in captivity.

Whale strandings on beaches are often pilot whales or other members of this group. No one knows why they swim up onto the beach, which often results in their death. There are lots of theories, but no solid evidence for the causes.

Minke whales

Minke whales are small rorqual whales, so they have baleen plates and throat pleats. They might be less exciting than other species, but are more likely to be seen than most. They breach less often than humpbacks and are smaller in length. Males are about 23' long and females about 3' longer. They are darkly colored: black, gray, or purple. Northern hemisphere minke whales have a band of white on their two pectoral fins making for easy identification. You can't see their baleen plates, but they have a lot of them. More than 300!

You can see them catch two or three breathes before arching their backs for a deep dive of 10 -20 minutes. They are long lived whales, with some reaching 60 years.

Minke whales are hunted today by Japan, Norway, and Iceland. Although all whaling is prohibited under the International Whaling Commission, those countries have special authorization for hunting a limited number of minkes. Japan claims to be conducting scientific research on the several hundred whales it catches each year, but no scientific results are published from this research. You can order whale meat in restaurants in Iceland and Norway or buy cans of whale meat in Japan. Please don't.

Fin whales

Greyhounds of the sea is the nickname given to these whales. They can sustain swimming speeds faster than your ship can go. Shorter than blue whales, they can be as long as 85'. They occur throughout the ocean and can be seen in groups of six or more.

A fin whale feeds near the surface. Photo by NOAA

Fin whales have several distinguishing features. Unlike humpbacks and blue whales, fin whales have a prominent dorsal fin. The fin is curved and it appears shortly after the blow. When they dive the flukes are rarely raised out of the water. They dive for about 15 minutes when feeding.

They have a pronounced splash guard around their twin blowholes. The blow is tall, although not as tall as a blue whale's. It can be 20' high.

The body is slender – appropriate for its nickname. The back is brown or gray. The undersides are noticeably lighter, almost white.

Notice the coloration of the head. Unlike other whales, the coloration is not symmetrical. The right side has a "jaw patch." This is an area of lighter coloration, light gray.

Sei whales

Smaller only than blue and fin whales, Sei whales can grow to 60' in length. They travel alone or in small pods throughout the ocean, although usually avoiding polar waters and tropical waters.

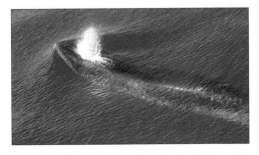

A Sei whale cruising along by itself. Photo by Sally Mizrock.

Sperm whales

Sperm whales are easy to identify. As a toothed whale they have a single blowhole. Unlike all other

The greyhound of the sea is the name given to fin whales. This one was heading towards its summer feeding grounds in Antarctica. Photo by Charles Ford.

A sperm whale blows. Note the blunt head and the angle of the blow. These distinctive features allow you to identify sperm whales. Photo by NOAA.

whales their blow is not vertical. It goes forward at a very discernible angle. The angle is about 45 degrees or halfway between vertical and horizontal. The head is squared off and it takes up about 1/3 of the animal's length. Instead of a dorsal fin, Sperm whales have a series of bumps along its back just in front of its huge flukes. Similar to right whales, sperm whales have wimpy pectoral fins.

The name sperm comes from the early misconception among whalers that the fluid inside the whale's head was semen. It was called spermaceti and was prized as a lubricant, candle wax, base for ointments, and antifreeze. One whale could yield 500 gallons of spermaceti. Pity the poor ship's boy who was lowered into the whales head to scoop out the precious material.

Not nearly as large as a blue whale, sperm whales can grow to 60'. They are the largest toothed animal, have the largest brain, and dive second deepest. Only Cuvier's beaked whales dive deeper.

Sperm whales eat squid, including giant squid. To catch their prey, they have to dive deep and stay down for up to an hour. They eat a lot. They consume about 3% of their body weight a day. Their daily diet includes about 3,000 pounds of squid with a few fish thrown in.

Sperm whale numbers are hard to pin down. Some estimates suggest there are more than 100,000 of them alive today.

Where to see whales

With more people on the water making observations we have discovered predictable migration routes as well as summer feeding grounds and winter birthing grounds for several species. gray whales travel along the U.S. west coast migrating annually from feeding grounds around Alaska and farther south to winter mating and birthing grounds in Baja California. Some 26,000 whales make the annual trip south in the fall and north in the spring.

Humpback whales live in both southern and northern hemispheres and don't seem to cross the equator. Groups seem to summer in one polar or sub-polar location and winter together in the tropics. You can find migration maps on line. A summer Alaska or Iceland cruise will give views of feeding and a February trip to Hawaii will reward you with great views during breeding. But there are many other locations around the world.

Once you have your itinerary do an on-line search for whale-watching tours in each port city you are visiting. Whether you intend to go on a tour or not, you can get valuable information on what you might see from the deck of your ship. The critical information is the list of species and time of year you can see them. Few places in the world offer year-round whale watching so dig down to find out if you will arrive when the whales are nearby. Of course if there is a naturalist on board he or she will love to tell you what to look for.

Here are some of the popular cruise areas with a listing of what you can see. Please understand the limitations of this listing. In no way is it complete. Many species are not on the list. Most sightings occur seasonally. I've listed the strongest seasonal predominance.

Alaska
- Beluga (Cook Inlet, Gulf of Alaska)
- Blue (Gulf of Alaska; July — August)
- Gray (summer)
- Humpback (summer)
- Minke
- Orca (summer)

Argentina
- Orca
- Southern right (October — December)

Australia
- Humpback
- Minke
- Pygmy right
- Southern right
- Sperm

Azores
- Humpback
- Orca
- Pilot
- Sperm
- White-beaked

Baja
- Blue
- Gray (winter)
- Humpback (winter)
- Minke

Bay of Biscay
- Pilot
- Sperm
- Fin
- Sei
- Minke
- Cuvier's beaked whales

British Isles
- Humpback
- Minke
- Orca

Canary Islands
- Short-finned pilot whales
- Bottlenose dolphins
- Brydes whales
- Blainville beaked whales
- Turtles: Green, loggerhead, Hawksbill, and leatherback

Caribbean
- Humpback (Dominican Republic)
- Sperm (Dominica)
- Turtles: Loggerhead, Hawksbill, Olive Ridley, and Green

French Polynesia
Humpback (June — October)
Pilot

Greenland
Beluga
Bowhead (Disko Bay; March - May)
Fin
Humpback
Minke

Hawaiian Islands
Humpback (November — April)
Orca
Short-fin pilot
Sperm

Iceland
Humpback
Minke
Orca (winter)
Blue
Fin
Sei

Indo-Pacific
Sperm whales

Mediterranean Sea
Fin whales
Sperm whales
Long-finned pilot whales
Cuvier's beaked whales

New England
Humpback
Northern right
Fin
Minke

New Zealand
Sperm (South Island)
Blue
Southern right
Humpback

Norwegian Coast
Beluga (far north)
Minke
Sperm (far north)
Orca
Humpback

Pacific Northwest
Gray
Humpback
Minke

Persian Gulf
Humpback dolphin
Bottlenose dolphin

South Africa
Southern right whales (June — November)
Humpbacks
Bottlenose dolphins

Southern California
Blue
Fin
Humpback

Western Pacific
Sperm

How to see whales

There are about 2 million whales in the world ocean. You're bound to see at least one. Persistence, luck, and knowing where to look are the keys to success. Did we mention luck?

If your ship is traveling at 20 knots and if visibility is good enough to see 2.5 miles on either side of the ship, on average you will pass one whale every 45 minutes or so. Unfortunately, the whales don't spread out evenly. Some places you might see twenty in an afternoon and other places you could look for days on end without seeing one.

To see whales, scan the water for the white vertical stream of a blow. Then use binoculars to see the features that identify the whale including body color, fin and fluke size and shape, and shape of the blow.

Scan the horizon. Then scan midway to the horizon. Then scan close by the ship. Repeat.

Binoculars are great, but not for finding whales. They are great for seeing the details once you know where to look.

Tell your eyes to look for spouts or splashes. Whales exhale in half a second or so, but their spout will hang in still air for several seconds. If you're lucky enough to be close, you might hear them breathe or even smell it. It smells like you'd expect for an animal that eats only seafood.

To maximize your chances, watch from the highest deck on the ship. This gives you the greatest visibility as height exposes more ocean surface. It also gives you wider lateral views than most of the lower decks and you can move from one side to the other quickly. And, more whale watchers will be on this deck so if one person sees a whale hopefully they will shout to alert others.

As you scan the sea your eyes will often see what appears to be a spout. Watch for a few seconds for another spout. Whales often travel with others so one spout will follow another. When whales travel by themselves you might have to wait 10 or 15 seconds to see the next spout.

Stand well forward on the deck. Standing near the stern guarantees you will get shorter glimpses of whales. As the ship steams along, you'll get only a few seconds of viewing. From a forward position you can see them farther away and as the ship approaches you'll get a longer view.

At sea the whales you see are probably traveling or migrating. They will spout, grab a breath, go under and come up again a few seconds later. If the ship disturbs them, they may dive and stay down longer.

Stand on the side opposite the sun. Give your eyeballs a break and don't fight the sun's glint.

If a whale is disturbed or is going down to feed, it will take a few breathes and then dive down usually with its tail fin, or fluke, held high. This makes a great camera shot or binocular view to identify the species. The shape and coloration of the tail can be enough to identify it.

Researchers use the markings on tails to identify individual animals.

I wish you good luck.

Whale FAQs

As you're standing on the deck looking for whales and talking to your shipmates someone will ask a question. Here are the answers for most of those questions.

Do ships ever hit whales? Unfortunately too often. A quick search of the internet will turn up photos of whales impaled on the front of ships.

Do whales sleep? Yes. They lie on the surface and some snore quite loudly. I woke a gray whale one morning in Southeast Alaska. Paddling my kayak I didn't see the whale lying low in the water, but when I got within 20', it awoke, smacked its flukes and took off. Kayaking near Cape Town, South Africa we paddled past two sleeping and snoring southern right whales. We were within a boat length of them and didn't wake them up. These whales were sleeping horizontally at the surface. Recently photos were taken of a pod of sperm whales sleeping below the surface with their bodies held vertically.

Are they fish? No, they are mammals. Like you and me they are warm blooded and breathe air. Hence you see them at the surface exhaling and taking a quick gulp of air before going down. If you're very close on a whale-watching trip you can hear them breathe and smell their fishy breath. Females bear live young that they nurse. Blue whale calves drink up to 150 gallons of super fat milk from their mothers each day.

Why do whales beach themselves? There are lots of theories, but no one knows for sure. It could be to escape something more frightening in the water. That could be human-generated sonar sounds or predators. Diseases are thought to cause a loss of direction and stranding. There could be several different reasons. We don't know.

Why do whales breach, spy hop (rise head first out of the water to look around), and slap their fins? We don't know, but if I could do that I certainly would.

Dolphins and porpoises

There are lots of them. There are more than 40 species of dolphins and 6 species of porpoise. Both are classified in the family Cetaceans with whales.

What's the difference between porpoise and dolphins? Porpoise are smaller, ranging in size from 4.5' to 7.5' and have blunt heads. Their teeth, if you get that close, are in the shape of a spade. They are most often seen one by itself. They tend to be shyer than dolphins. Most live near shore.

Dolphin, but not porpoise, will play in the bow wave of a ship. Ryan Bent Photography.

Dolphins and porpoise are mammals and must come to the surface to breathe. Both groups of animals are toothed whales so they have a single blow hole. Photo by Will Hayes.

Dolphins are larger from 5' to over 30' in length (only the orca get this big). Their heads narrow often to a pronounced beak and their teeth are conical. If you are in the middle of an ocean, you are more likely to see dolphins. Dolphins are often seen in large pods. Some species will approach a ship and perform or play in the ship's bow wave.

Both dolphins and porpoise eat fish and squid. Both are intelligent animals.

How to see dolphins

Look for the white splashes as they break the surface while swimming. If the winds are over 17 knots and generating whitecaps, it is very difficult to see these splashes

A pod of pantropical spotted dolphins leaps out of the water. Photo by NOAA.

unless they are close to the ship. It is unlikely you will see their blows. If you are close you might hear them breathe. Some dolphins will pay no attention to the ship, but many will swim over to investigate or to play with it.

Off the west coast of Mexico, a pod of dolphins keeps up with our ship.

With the ship speeding along to make the next port in time, sightings at sea are short-lived. Some dolphin species like to swim in the bow wave of ships. As the ship approaches them they will swim out of the way and then circle around and join the ship.

The most acrobatic dolphin are spinners. Typically they perform behind the ship in spectacular displays of jumping and spinning. They travel in pods of a dozen up to a thousand. They often leap vertically out of the water and spin once or twice between crashing back into the water. Photo by Will Hayes.

Unfortunately, on many large ships it's impossible to get a good view of them once they are swimming under the bow. However, as they race to get to the bow wave and fall back from the bow you can look straight down to see them underwater. As they rise, they open their blowhole, spout, and get a quick gulp of air. Set your camera on continuous mode and hope. Dolphin can swim faster than the ship, but can't maintain high speeds for long.

Some of the best places to see dolphin swimming at the bow are in fjords and coming in and out of port. For example Rangiroa, the largest atoll in the Tuamotu group in the South Pacific, has a narrow passage from the sea into the lagoon. A resident pod of dolphin joins ships entering and leaving the lagoon. If you're a diver this is a great place to dive with dolphins as well as see them from the deck.

Some dolphins will prefer to play in the ships wake. You don't get to see them for long as the ship quickly pulls away from them.

One good indication that dolphin are present is swarming birds. If there are lots of birds diving in one area, something is in the water concentrating fish and driving them to the surface. Often that something is dolphins. Feeding whales will also attract sea birds as will a school of fish attacking smaller fish.

Have the camera ready because you will have only fractions of a second to get great shots like this. Photo by Will Hayes.

A pink dolphin jumps out of the Rio Negro on an Amazon River Cruise. Photo by Bill Yeaton.

Have your camera ready for taking bursts of photos. Hopefully one image will be clear enough to identify the dolphin by their coloration. Check guide books for suggestions of what species might be in your location.

Some dolphins hang out with whales and seem to play with them. Best documented are bottlenose dolphins being lifted out of the water by humpback whales. Others have been observed surfing on the bow wave of a blue whale. Dolphins are notoriously promiscuous and interact with other species in unexpected ways.

Marine birds

Marine birds, correctly identified as pelagic birds, live on the ocean. You can see shore birds at sea, but rarely do you see them out of sight of land. Marine birds can be seen in the most remote areas of the world ocean.

Leaning over the side of a boat gave a great view of this dolphin. The single blow hole is visible as this dolphin leaps out of the water off Baja. Photo by Barbara Sobey.

Most spectacular are spinner dolphin. These mammals are 6 – 7' long. They like to jump vertically out of the water and spin around a vertical axis, before flopping back into the water. They travel in groups of 100 to 1,000 animals so you can see dozens of these acrobats jumping and spinning at the same time. They prefer to jump behind the ship. For some reason we tend to see them around noon, as we were eating lunch on the top deck restaurant at the stern.

The word pelagic refers to the sea. Pelagic birds spend their lives at sea and may come ashore only to breed.

Cormorants need to dry their wings as they don't have as much oil in their feathers as do other diving birds.

Occasionally you will see land birds on a ship in the middle of the ocean. Some get blown off course while migrating and land on ships when they are too exhausted to fly farther. We once sailed from San Diego with a peregrine falcon on board. We didn't notice the bird for a few days, but then we saw it every day perched high on the ships superstructure. Unlike most land birds at sea the falcon was able to find food. We watched it catch flying fish and eat them on the wing before landing back on the ship. When we made the first port-of-call in Nuka Hiva, the falcon jumped ship. On other voyages we've found land birds so exhausted that they allowed us to approach closely. There's nothing to do for them but appreciate the distant flights they must have made.

The largest group of pelagic birds includes albatrosses, petrels, and shearwaters. There are many species in this group so we won't try to name them. They range in size from the largest bird on the planet, the Wandering Albatross with a 12' wing span, to some of the smaller birds, storm petrels that can hover in flight to pick up food on the surface of the sea.

Albatross especially spend long periods of time at sea. They can go years before touching land. Like other birds they need water to survive. They and other pelagic birds ingest salt water with their food and expel the salt through a pair of openings on their bills. The salt is removed from their blood by a gland above their eyes. If you get close enough you can see salt crystals below the openings on the bills.

They discourage predators, or humans who get too close, by projectile vomiting a vile fluid. You have been warned, stay away.

Not a pelagic bird, bald eagles are seen along the inside passage and elsewhere near shore. Photo by Rob Avery.

Pelagic birds feed mostly on squid, fish, and small animals. Some dive for food and some scavenge from the ocean surface.

Some of the larger members of this group can hold their wings outstretched without using their muscles. They lock their wings in place so they don't exert energy in flight. To gain lift they use dynamic soaring (described below).

They fly constantly, awake or asleep. Flapping their wings to stay aloft would require more energy (food) than large pelagic birds can find at sea. So, they glide using the wind rather than flapping their wings.

Pelagic birds are long lived with the documented record being well over 66 years. Wisdom, a female Laysan Albatross, has been tagged several times in her life so we know she is at least 66 years old.

Looking at pelagic birds sitting on the water notice how high they sit. Their feathers are waterproof and they hold a lot of air. Compare their height in the water to cormorants, which are coastal birds or aquatic birds. Cormorants sit quite low in the water. Their wings are not waterproof and they hold much less air, so they have less "freeboard." That is, they sit lower in the water. This gives cormorants an advantage diving since they don't have to fight the buoyancy other birds do. And

A flat rock makes a good location for drying wings for these shags. Shags and cormorants are part of a group of 40 bird species. Photo by Barbara Sobey.

it explains why you so often see cormorants, but not other birds, drying their wings in the sun as they sit on pilings and buoys.

Pelagic birds face several human-caused threats including fishing long-lines. Birds eat the bait on the hooks and get caught. Many ingest plastic that fills their guts, blocks their digestive system, and provides no nutrition. Pesticides and other organic pollutants adhere to the bits of plastic birds eat so the plastic pollution is even more dangerous for them. Natural threats include land predators predating in colonies and larger birds at sea. No wonder pelagic bird populations are today only 10% of what they were 50 years ago

A beautiful blue-eyed cormorant or an Imperial Shag. These birds are found in southern South America where they dive down to about 80' to catch small fish. Photo by Charles Ford.

How to see pelagic birds

To view pelagic birds you need a good pair of binoculars with stabilization. You don't use the binoculars to spot the birds, but once you spot them with naked eyeballs, binoculars help you see the details that can help identify them.

Shearwaters

Watching from just aft of the bow you can see graceful shearwaters crossing the bow, low to the water. More often you can see them at the waist of the ship. As you look out about 200m from the ship you'll see stiff winged birds flying low to the surface. You will lose sight of them as they turn the dark tops of their wings toward you only to re-appear moments later as they expose their white undersides. It looks like their wings are about to touch or shear the waves. They turn side to side as they weave their way between successive waves in a ballet on the undulating sea.

Their stiff wings save energy. They don't flap, they extend their

Brown boobies are a common sight at sea. Photo by Will Hayes.

Gannets often use ships to frighten flying fish into flight. This gannet was photographed in New Zealand by Charles Ford.

Thousands of nesting gannets adorn this small rock off Alderney, Channel Islands. The noise and smell are distinctive. Photo by Barbara Sobey.

wings and lock them in place so they fly with little muscle power. How do they keep up with the ship and rarely flap their wings? That is the awesomeness of dynamic soaring, explained below.

Gannets and boobies

Back to the bow. Higher, often directly above the bridge, is where boobies and gannets will fly. Watch them carefully as they too keep up with the ship without flapping their wings.

As the ship moves forward it pushes the air in front up and over the hull. This mass of rising air gives lift to the birds. If you've ever dreamed of flying you will enjoy this vicarious pleasure. Birds on land do the same thing using winds pushed up by hills and mountains. Sea gulls glide over the roof of buildings on the up-rushing air.

Gannets are closely related to boobies. Like boobies they dive for their food. They nest on isolated

There are ten species of boobies. This is the masked booby as you can see its black mask. Booby was a derogatory name meaning "stupid" as the birds didn't recognize human hunters as a threat. Photo by Will Hayes.

The most colorful fliers are the red-footed (shown here) and blue-footed boobies. Boobies dive for food. Starting high above the water they fold their wings at the last second as they crash into the ocean. Air sacs in their face help cushion the blow. Photo by Will Hayes

Comical is the description most often given to these birds. A trip to the Galapagos Islands will reward you with opportunities to capture them on film. Photo by Charles Ford.

rocks to lay their egg and tend their offspring.

Of course these bow-wave-riding birds are not just hitching a ride. They are waiting for the ship to startle flying fish into flight. When a fish takes off a bird will turn, pull in its wings, and dive to give chase. Sometimes it will catch a fish in the air but more often it will dive into the water to catch it.

You will know when it has caught a fish as it will take a few seconds to swallow (and possibly savor) its meal. By the time it takes to the air again, the ship will be far ahead, and it will have to work hard flapping its wings to catch up.

Easy to recognize are frigate birds. The shape of their wings and tail are a given away. Photo by Will Hayes.

Frigate birds

Sometimes you will see magnificent frigate birds flying even higher, above the boobies and gannets. These are the pirates of the sea, robbing the smaller birds of their catch. When a booby dives to catch a

This frigate rested on the mast of our ship. It waited there until it saw a booby catching a flying fish and then it took to wing to scare the booby into giving up its catch. Photo by Will Hayes.

A magnificent frigate bird is chasing a brown booby that just caught fish. The frigate will try to steal the fish from the booby. Photo by Will Hayes.

fish, a frigate bird will follow to steal the fish from it.

More often you see frigate birds as the ship approaches land. Entering and leaving the Panama Canal almost guarantees several sightings.

These large-winged birds get lift by riding rising air currents caused by solar heating of the land surface. They ride higher and higher and then head out to sea to steal or catch their food. You can identify these prehistoric looking birds by their large body size, pterodactyl-like wings, long hooked bill, and forked tail.

Dynamic soaring

Birds flying at the bow use the updraft of wind from the ship to stay aloft without flapping. At the waist of the ship (mid-ship) or behind the ship you can gaze out to see shearwaters on stiff wings grazing the tops of waves. They will skim so close to the surface that you're sure they will touch a wave. Flying along the trough of a wave they are shielded from the wind. Watch as they fly up, out of the trough, over top of a wave to catch the full force of the breeze. The onrushing wind hitting the underside of their wings pushes them quickly skyward. Once they have gained elevation, they turn downwind and glide amongst the following waves.

This is dynamic soaring. Many pelagic birds use the technique rather than flapping wings to generate lift. I once watched an albatross follow my navy ship. We were steaming at 18 knots in the South Pacific. The bird kept up with us for at least half an hour without once flapping its wings.

Albatross

Albatross are the ultimate design in pelagic birds. In their environment of high and continuous winds they thrive where other species fail. Without strong winds, they would have to flap their wings to move and feed. Undoubtedly they would not be able to find enough food to survive the high energy demands of flying. They are perfectly designed for their

Majestic flyers wandering albatrosses spend most of their life in solitary flight on the ocean. Photo by Charles Ford.

environment and poorly designed for any other.

Watch for albatross in the wake of the ship. You're more likely to see them in the South Pacific, South Atlantic, and Southern Indian Oceans at higher latitudes. But others do live in the northern hemisphere. None at the equator. Equatorial winds are too light and variable to support these magnificent birds.

Stop on the fantail or back of the ship and watch the white wake of the ship. As albatross or other birds fly back and forth over the wave you will see their dark wing tops in contrast to the white wake. When they turn

showing their white undersides they will disappear from view. They usually don't get close to the ship so a pair of binoculars would help. They are looking for squid or small fish that have been disorientated or even killed by the ship passing overhead.

Fulmar

Fulmars are pelagic birds that come ashore only to breed. They look like coastal-hugging sea gulls, but unlike gulls they fly like pelagic

Skuas are kleptoparasites. They rob food from other birds. They are commonly seen in the polar regions and sub-polar regions. Photo by Barbara Sobey

birds. That is, they seldom flap their wings and instead fly stiff-winged using dynamic soaring to gain altitude. Fulmars breed in huge colonies. They eat squid, fish, and whatever else they can scavenge from the sea.

Pelicans

Not pelagic birds, pelicans should not be included with the others. But pelicans are too cool to leave out. They live in coastal waters and catch

Fulmar looks like gulls, but are pelagic birds with salt-ejecting tubes in their beaks. Photo by Charles Ford.

These large birds have long bills. Pelicans are land-based but are often seen at sea, near shore, diving from great heights. Photo by Will Hayes.

fish on the surface or they dive from great heights, kicking up big splashes, to chase fish underwater.

These are easy to identify as they are big birds with enormous bills. They float high in the water due to air sacs in their body. The air sacs may also cushion their impact with the water when they dive. They live in warm regions throughout the world.

They are easiest to spot when they are diving for fish. Often you can see dozens of pelicans diving and splashing in the same location.

Galapagos penguins live farther north than any other species. Photo by Charles Ford.

The waters near Antarctica are home to several species of penguins including these chinstrap penguins. Photo take near South Shetland Island by Charles Ford.

Penguins

These flightless birds use their wings to fly through the water. Steered by their feet they can travel at speeds up to 17 miles per hour. Usually they swim at slower speeds.

You can see them in select locations around the world. Most penguin areas are in the southern hemisphere, but some Galapagos penguins live just north of the equator in those islands. Cape Town is a great region to see them. If you're on a ship's excursion there you might see them swimming near shore or along the beach, hiding from the sun in the bushes.

Off the southeast coast of Australia and off the eastern side of New Zealand's' South Island you find fairy penguins. A cruise around the southern end of South America and along the Chilean coast provides opportunities The Falklands, South Georgia Island, and the Antarctic Peninsula are rich in penguin life.

Storm Petrels

Much smaller than most pelagic birds, storm petrels can hover above

We found this storm petrel on the deck. Often these small birds are found in shock on the deck, unable it seems to fly away. I release them over the side and nearly always they fly successfully. You can see the small tubes on its beak where it extrudes excess salt as do many pelagic birds. Photo by Barbara Sobey.

Puffins are pelagic birds that breed in large colonies on shore and catch food by diving. Photo by Rob Avery.

the surface and pick up bits of food. They walk across the ocean surface while flapping their wings. The name Petrel is derived from St. Peter and his walk on the sea. These small birds often collide with the ship and can be found on deck.

Pelagic bird breeding

The birds in this group form long-term pair bonds, some species bond for life. Most lay one egg per year and some breed less frequently. Nearly all breed in large colonies ashore. For some, like the Wandering Albatross, breeding in their home colony is the only time in their lives they touch land. Just outside the port of Dunedin, New Zealand is a colony of royal albatross that can been seen from cruise ships.

Puffins

Puffins are favorites for many marine observers. Small, stubby bodied with short wings and tail, they flap like crazy to lift off the water. Young puffins not yet able to fly will

flee an approaching ship by slapping their wings on the water. Not great fliers, they are great divers. They eat small fish, most especially sand eels that they carry in their bills. These popular birds are found in the North Pacific and North Atlantic Oceans.

Bird identification

Most ship libraries will have one or two guides for birds of the cruising region or the world ocean. If the internet is working, try the Cornell University guide, allaboutbirds.org. Another site is ebird.org

I usually find someone aboard who knows a lot more about seabirds than I do. Such experts are easy to spot as they stand on deck with binoculars raised. A friendly "what do you see" usually opens a dialog that can last the duration of the cruise.

Seals and sea lions

In the water these animals can be difficult to spot. You can see them in some ports swimming around ships. At sea you might see a dark

Fur seals and sea lions are hard to distinguish. They live in cool to cold water and are best seen when hauled out of the water. Photo by Rob Avery.

Sea lions enjoying the sun. Unlike seals, sea lions often climb out of the water. Here they are resting on floats with nets to hold small fish in an aquaculture operation in Mexico. Photo by Barbara Sobey.

head emerge or see one swimming. Better views are afforded at "haul-outs." These are usually small islands that the animals use for sun bathing, mating, and pupping. You definitely need binoculars to see these animals.

To distinguish between a seal and sea lion, look first at the head. Sea lions have external or outer ears; seals do not. The front flippers on a sea lion are quite large. In the water they propel the animal. On land, they prop up their bodies so their head is above the ground. Sea lions can walk with these front flippers.

Seals have short front flippers that provide steering underwater and are nearly useless on land. They lie on the beach with their heads in the sand or on the rocks or ice. Moving on land is arduous for seals. In the water they are masters of movement. Hence, they spend most of the time in the water.

Sea lions are noisy. Sail into Astoria, Oregon and you'll hear their

Large seals living along the coast of England, Scotland, Orkney Islands, Norway, and the Baltic Sea. Along the western side of the North Atlantic they inhabit areas from New Jersey northward.

Harbor seals are smaller members of this group. They live close to shore in cooler waters. Photo by Rob Avery.

barking anywhere in the city. Seals are quiet. Seals tend to be solitary and sea lions can be found in large groups.

Fur seals are closely related to sea lions. At a distance it can be difficult to tell them apart.

Smaller than sea lions fur seals have larger front flippers, shorter noses, and larger external ears. Fur seal males can be as much as five time larger than females. This sexual dimorphism can help to distinguish them.

Gray seals

In the colder waters of the North Atlantic and North Pacific gray or grey seals are common. These are large animals, with males growing as long as 10'. You can distinguish them from other seals by the shape of their head. They look like a dog with a long snout.

They eat fish, octopus, and crabs. They are quite uninhibited about jumping up onto a dock or boat to beg to be fed.

A sea otter with pup in Alaska. Photo by Rob Avery.

Harbor seals

Harbor seals are commonly seen in harbors and near ports. They are the most widely distributed member of the pinniped family that includes seals, sea lions, and walruses. They live solitary lives except when moulting or breeding ashore. White sharks and orca prey on harbor seals.

Sea otter

What a special treat it is to see sea otter. Although they were widely distributed the range of sea otters is now quite restricted. You can see

Life looks easy when you are a sea otter. Photo by Will Hayes.

them along the Washington coast up to Alaska in the Inside Passage. There are also some along the coast of California.

Otter are amazing animals. Unlike other marine mammals they don't have a thick protective layer of body fat. They have their rich fur to keep them warm and they need to generate body heat. That means they have to eat. They eat 25% of the body weight a day. Maybe the same percentage people do on a cruise ship. They eat fish, shell fish, crabs, and sea urchins.

Sea otter played a major role in the development of Alaska. They were the magnet that first drew explorers and hunters to this land.

To see them look for the frons of kelp. With binoculars scan the floating frons. Otters like to wrap frons around them to hold them in place. If you're very lucky you might see one cracking open a clam or caring for a baby.

Flying fish

Watch the sea explode as a school of flying fish takes off and flies across the water for 200m. It is a magnificent sight and one too many ocean travelers never see.

My first encounter with flying fish was aboard a World War II era freighter in the western Pacific. An early morning walk on the deck brought me face to fin with several fish that had unfortunately landed on our deck. The deck was at least 20 feet above the sea surface so the fish had gotten some good air to land aboard.

Flying fish fly to avoid predators. They accelerate with just a few fast flicks of their tail to erupt from the water and, hopefully, bewilder that bigger fish chasing them. Most often from the deck of the ship you see flying fish startled by the ship, not

In tropical waters where you might not see a lot of other marine life, flying fish will appear. Watch as they take off when the ship approaches. They glide for dozens of yards before swishing their tails in the water to gain extra propulsion. Photo by Will Hayes.

other fish, but either way it is a grand show.

The ship's bow wave or shadow startles the fish to flight. Dolphin (the fish), tuna, swordfish, marlin and other large carnivorous fish feed on flying fish. They usually catch them in the water, but sometimes leap up to catch them in mid-air.

Boobies, gannets, and other marine birds take advantage of the ship scaring flying fish. As the flying fish startle and take off into the air, the birds dive and snag them. Sometimes you can see the birds catching them in flight. More often the birds crash into the sea a half second behind the fish and catch the prey underwater. Keeping score on the deck you know the bird has won if it comes up to the surface, shakes its head to align the fish in its throat so it slides down easily.

The birds not only get an almost free lunch from the ship scaring the fish into flight, they also get a free ride. Watch them glide above bridge traveling at the speed of the ship without using flapping their wings. As the ship speeds forward it pushes up the air in front of it providing a cushion of uprising air to support the birds.

Watch closely as the flying fish take off. They spread their pectoral fins, the fins on each side of the fish. Some species of flying fish have two pectoral fins and others have four. Some are only a few inches long and others are up to a foot and a half.

Flying fish don't really fly. They glide on the lift provided by their outstretched pectoral fins. They don't flap these fins, but use them like the wings of a glider. They can glide about 5 feet for every foot of elevation they lose falling back to the sea. Their 5:1 glide ratio compares poorly to the greatest ocean flyer, the great albatross, 20:1. But those giants are full-time flyers that spend years at sea without touching land. A more realistic comparison is to the small marine birds petrels. Their glide ratio is about 4:1. A sea gull about 11:1. A 747 glides 15 feet for every foot it loses in altitude. So, from an aerodynamic point of view, 5:1 for a flying fish isn't bad at all.

They do glide farther than the glide ratio suggests. Because they fly so close to the sea surface they benefit from "ground effect." Airplanes, birds, and flying fish get extra lift and

Flying fish jump out of the water and glide. If they need to go farther to evade predators they dip their tail fin into the water and wiggle it quickly. Photo by NOAA.

decreased drag when they are flying close to the surface.

A quick calculation shows how important ground effect is. Flying fish usually rise 4 or 5 feet above the ocean surface. With a 5:1 glide ratio they could travel at most 25'. But your eyes tell you they are going much farther than that.

Sharp eyes or good binoculars or a camera lens will reveal another secret of flying fish. Unlike the tails of most fish, flying fish tails are not symmetric. The bottom half or lobe is much larger than the top half. Watching the fish skim across the water gives a clue to why this asymmetry is advantageous.

A flying fish erupts from the water at about 37 miles per hour. It stays close to the surface to take advantage of ground effect. Sometimes a gust of wind can launch it to greater heights so it can land on the deck of a ship, but usually it stays close. As it glides along it loses elevation just as an airliner does when the engines are cut back for landing. But then the magic occurs.

You'll see the fish tip the lower lobe of its tail in the water and wiggle it back and forth. It wiggles too fast to see each movement – about 70 wiggles per second – but it leaves a wake in the water you can see. And, you'll notice that the rapid tail movements thrust it higher above the sea.

With the additional altitude it can glide farther. It can do this tail wiggle several times to extend its flight to up to 400m. With some luck it will have flown far away whatever was chasing it.

There are more than 60 species of flying fish. You'll see them in tropical and subtropical waters. Sometimes two or three species live in the same

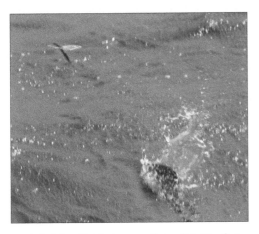

A dolphin (fish) chases a flying fish. The flying fish leap out of the water and glide to escape predators. Photo by Will Hayes.

area. They feed on small animals that live in the upper layers of the ocean. They are eaten by lots of bigger fish and humans.

The national dish of Barbados is the flying fish. The image of a flying fish adorns their one dollar coin. Unfortunately, they love eating the fish too much. The fishery surrounding the island nation is empty and they have to import their fish or send their fishing boats far away from Barbados to catch them.

How to see flying fish

In warm waters even if you can't see anything else, you can see flying fish. You'll find them in most tropical and subtropical waters. Go forward on any weather deck – any deck exposed to the weather. The highest deck provides the broadest view so start there. A lower promenade deck affords a closer view of the take-off, but poor angle for landings.

The shady side of the ship gives you better visibility as you're not peering into the sun. Go forward so you are just above the start of the ship's bow wave. Flying fish usually launch where they first encounter the ship – its bow wave or its shadow. When they start their flight they are usually within 50' of the ship.

After five minutes if you haven't seen any, walk aft. Sometimes the first ship-generated wave doesn't cause them to jump, but something farther aft will.

Flying fish travel in schools so you might not see any for a long time and then suddenly see one flight after another.

While you're looking for flying fish, keep an eye out for pelagic birds, especially boobies and gannets. If you see them flying above the forward part of the ship, go watch. They can drop a stinky mess of guano on the deck so don't stand directly beneath them. If there are flying fish about you will see the birds peel off to give chase. As one fish jumps out of the water one bird will pull in its outstretched wings and dive like a fighter pilot. It will get behind the fish and if lucky, snag it before it lands back into the water. Otherwise it will dive into the sea following the fish.

Keep watching as the ship steams by. The bird will come to the surface, swallow the fish if it got one, and then laboriously launch itself back into the air. Eventually it will catch up with the ship and take its place waiting in line for its next meal.

Sea turtles

Seven species of these reptiles still live in the ocean. Most often you find them close to shore, but some do swim across the ocean to nest so it's possible to find them mid-ocean.

As they are reptiles they breathe air. They can stay underwater for several hours when they are sleeping. While finding food they may stay down 20 – 40 minutes.

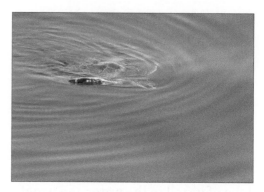

There are many thousands of sea turtles so your patience can be rewarded with a sighting from your ship or boat. Photo by Will Hayes.

Most of the species are found exclusively in tropical water. They are cold-blooded and don't do well in colder water. The exception is the leatherback. They have some control over body temperature and can maintain a temperate 32° Fahrenheit higher than the water temperature. Leatherbacks can survive nicely at higher latitudes. They are constantly on the go spending less than two minutes a day resting. They eat jellyfish and must consume a lot of them to get enough nourishment. They are the fastest reptile in the world with a top speed in excess of 20 miles per hour. These are giants,

Females lay about 100 eggs in nests they dig in sandy beaches. They lay several times a season about 2 or more weeks apart.

with the largest weighing in at over 1,000 pounds.

In Hawaii especially you are likely to see green turtles. As adults they are vegetarians eating sea grasses and algae, that turns their body fat green. Juveniles are omnivores as are many of the other turtles throughout their lives.

Loggerhead turtles are found in tropical and subtropical waters. They eat bottom dwelling (benthic) animals in shallow water and jellyfish in the deeper ocean. Like the other sea turtles they don't go ashore, except the females to lay eggs.

Hawksbill turtles eat sponges and other benthic animals. The other species of sea turtles are olive ridley (found in tropical waters), Kemp's ridley (found along the western North Atlantic Ocean shore), and Flatblack (found exclusively around Australia and New Guinea).

How to see sea turtles

Like your fellow passengers, sea turtles like to bask in the warmth of the tropical sun. All except for the leatherback will snooze on the ocean surface. You can't see them far from the ship as their shells rise only a few inches above the surface, so you might have better viewing on the promenade deck where you are closer to the water. Look for a 3' diameter brown disk. If the ship wakes one up, it will raise its head to

After digging a nest, laying her eggs, and covering her nest, a female laboriously crawls back to the sea. They need to get back to the cooling waters of the ocean before the sun rises too high in the sky. Otherwise they overheat and can die on the beach.

In warm waters you can see sea turtles sunning themselves at the surface. Look close to the ship with the sun at your back. Once startled by the ship they will dive. Photo by Will Hayes.

I watch an olive ridley dig her nest. Our group of university students learned how to make and record measurements on the egg-laying turtles and then spent several hours after dark collecting as much data as possible. Photo by Matt Corliss.

see what's causing the disturbance. A second later it will dive to get away.

Out of every 10 turtle observations, you might see one pair of turtles mating. The male will be on top and the poor female underneath looks like she can barely get a breath of air. Mating pairs tend to concentrate on their pursuits and pay little attention to the passing ship.

Ashore you can see females coming ashore to lay their eggs generally in the late summer to fall season. Each species is different, but they lay

Swim with the turtles

You can snorkel with sea turtles in many places around the world. They won't bother you and generally will avoid you in the water. If you approach them slowly and don't get too close they will pay little attention to you. Once disturbed, however, they will swim away. They don't look nimble, but they can fly underwater. Don't grab their shell. Just enjoy a natural encounter.

about 100 eggs in a nest they build in the beach. They cover the nest and try to camouflage it so land predators can't find it. The eggs incubate for a few weeks. Warm temperatures in the nest cause the hatchlings to turn out female and cooler temperatures cause them to become males. You have to wonder what effects global warming will have on their species survival.

Baby turtles break out of their shell, dig out of their nest, and make

This green turtle didn't pay much attention to me as I got close enough to take some photographs. Green turtles can be found many places including just outside the cruise ship terminal on Barbados where I took this photo.

a mad dash to the sea. Gulls, vultures, and land animals have a feast on the ones that are slow. Once at sea the little guys are a favorite prey for many animals. They have to hide in floating seaweed until they are large enough to better defend themselves. Even adults are taken by sharks, but some recent observations show how clever they can be to avoid even the largest predator. As a shark comes in to munch on the horizontally swimming turtle, it executes a sharply banked turn. The shark can't bite the now vertically-orientated shell and can't turn as sharply, so it swims past. After several failed attempts, the shark goes on to find an easier meal.

Arribada

A few years ago I led sixteen university students to the University of Costa Rica research facility at Ostional Beach on the Pacific Coast. We were participating in a research project that involved measuring female olive ridley turtles when they came ashore to lay eggs. We counted the eggs they laid and placed metal tags on their flippers. Instead of the few dozen we were expecting to find so late in the nesting season, 71,000 turtles came ashore in one night. This was an "arribada" (arrival).

A few times a year on a few different beaches olive ridley females come ashore in vast numbers. We were operating in the dark as lights disturb the turtles laying eggs. Turtle after turtle laboriously waddled up the beach, crawling over each other

During an arribada most of the female turtles come ashore after dark. As the sun sets along this beach in Costa Rica the vanguard starts to arrive. Over 70,000 turtles came ashore this night along 900m of beach.

The Sargasso Sea in the Atlantic Ocean is named for the floating plants, Sargassum. The Sargasso itself is unique as it is the only sea that is not contained by any land features. Instead its boundaries are four ocean currents.

and our undergraduate students if they didn't get out of the way. Each turtle would dig its nest and as often as not would dig up the nest from an earlier-arriving turtle.

If you have the opportunity to witness an arribada on your world travels, I strongly suggest you do. In my mind it ranks up with seeing humpback whales breach or eagles catch fish on the fly. A video tape recording doesn't capture the awe; you have to experience it.

Seaweed

When we think of plants on land we think of trees, crops, flowers, and bushes. All are firmly anchored to the ground. Roots provide water and nutrients. A vascular system delivers these throughout the plant. They grow slowly, taking a season or years to reach maturity. In the ocean plants are predominately microscopic, free floating plankton (meaning wanderers). They lack roots and vascular systems, and they grow and reproduce quickly.

There are some marine plants, like kelp, that are anchored to the bottom in shallow water. These are held in place by "holdfasts," not roots. Nutrients are available for all cells in the surrounding seawater so there is no need to move them through a vascular system. These plants are limited to depths shallow enough for the holdfasts to anchor the plant while allowing the leaves or blades to gather sunlight for photosynthesis. Their range is very limited.

Another group of plants float along the surface and are large enough to see from a ship. These are Sargassum. No roots, no holdfasts, just floating plants.

The floating Sargassum provides safe havens for many animals including this baby hawksbill turtle. You can see these plants in tropical seas. Photo by NOAA.

The plant Sargassum is found throughout the ocean. When the wind blows at just the right speed to create windrows, the Sargassum lines up in parallel lines.

Nautical lore says that sailing ships could get entangled in the Sargassum. Your ship, however, will power right through. The clumps of Sargassum are entire communities of plants and animals. Fish, crabs, and other marine life live in or beneath the clumps. Baby sea turtles hide

in the clumps. If you ever have the opportunity (with a facemask) to examine floating Sargassum you are likely to find a host of other life attached or hiding nearby.

The Sargassum are not just found in the Sargasso Sea. Anywhere in the tropical or subtropical Atlantic Ocean, including the Gulf of Mexico will have some. In other oceans related species float on the surface.

Plankton

Phytoplankton—microscopic plants – power the ocean food webs. Like land plants we're familiar with they convert solar energy into food energy and feed all the animals of the sea. Being microscopic there are hard to see from the deck of a ship.

When they bloom, however, they are present in such vast quantities that they color the ocean surface. Swirls of green or red or brown make the ocean look like a 70s paisley shirt.

They bloom naturally, but also bloom when nutrients run off land and overwhelm the marine system. Think of a million lawn-mower-Larrys over fertilizing their yards with the runoff washing into the streams, rivers, and ocean. Once in the ocean this unnatural abundance of fertilizer causes plants to grow at excessive speed and to die before being eaten by animals. Bacteria decay the plants, robbing the water of its oxygen and creating zones of the sea that cannot support animal life. Such regions are dead zones.

When these blooms hurt other marine organisms, or us humans, we call this a Harmful Algae Bloom. The old term for harmful algae bloom was red tide. High concentrations of algae cause the plants to release toxins that can kill the animals that eat them. Or, these toxins can bio accumulate in each succeeding higher trophic level. Oysters or muscles accumulate the toxins. When we sit down to eat a dozen oysters, we have just bio-accumulated lots of toxins. Instead if we're lucky the harmful algae bloom has been discovered before the oysters are harvested and before we eat them. These blooms shut down local and regional oyster industries every year.

Harmful or not, you can see the blooms on the surface and can marvel at how many million plant cells are in each gallon of seawater.

Jellyfish

A common sighting at sea, jellyfish occur everywhere in the ocean. It is usually the large circular bell that you see. These can be cloudy white or brown circles, just below the surface. Usually when you see one, you will see many.

The jellyfish stream long tentacles loaded with stinging cells. When something bumps into a stinging cell, the cell fires a tiny dart. Attached to the dart is a tube through which the cell pumps a toxin. They eat mostly plankton, small fish, and other jellyfish. Some fish and sea turtles eat them.

There's not much to these animals. They are 95% water. But they can do real damage. Blooms of jellyfish clog the water intakes of power plants and reverse osmosis water plants. Several scientists contend that there is a global explosion of jellyfish, but there isn't much data yet to support this idea.

You can also see the much smaller purple "by-the-wind sailors" or Velella on the surface. Jellyfish will be below the surface while Velella are floating on the surface. Velella are a small disk an inch or two in diameter with a rigid sail that stands above the surface vertically one inch. Onshore winds sometimes fill beaches with Velella.

Chapter 5
Ship, Ahoy!

S POTTING ANOTHER SHIP MAKES THE SEA DAY more fun. If you're traveling along a shipping route, you will see many. Crossing the ocean between two smaller ports will make a ship sighting the observational highlight of the day. Most of the ships or other technology that you will see at sea fall into one of these major classes.

Aids to navigation

Buoys are easy to spot as you approach port. Some buoys mark the channel and others mark reefs all ships should avoid.

Range markers are used along rivers and fjords. These are triangular or rectangular signs, one above and a few hundred meters behind the other. The signs have two or three panels with different colors to catch you eye. Often the outer panels are painted white and the inner panel is black. The pilot or ship's officer maneuvers the ship so the two signs are aligned vertically. When they are aligned, the ship is in the channel.

Channel marking buoy. Buoys are numbered so the first buoy you encounter coming from the sea to shore is number 1. Odd buoys are on one side of the channel and even buoys are on the other side. Each buoy's position is marked on navigational charts.

On the island of Alderney, part of the Channel Islands, this range marker guides ships into safe moorage. To use a range marker sailors aligned two identical markers, one above the other mounted on shore.

This ship lays cable off its bow for communications and data transmission.

A buoy graveyard or repair yard in Le Havre, France.

Every nation that uses aids to navigation has to repair and replace the buoys. That is the job of buoy tenders. They have a working deck forward of the bridge and have a crane to lift buoys on board. This is a Chinese buoy tender.

Cable layers

To get data and communications around the world without relying on satellites, companies use subsea fiber optic cables. To lay the cables requires specialized ships. The clue to their identification is a reel either at the bow or stern that guides the cable overboard and into the sea. There are about 60 cable layers.

Coast Guard ships

The Coast Guard has a variety of vessels including ice breakers, cutters, buoy tenders, tugs, and other support ships. Ice breakers have red hulls and the cutwater (leading edge of the bow) angles down and backward to allow the ship to ride up onto sea ice to break it. The superstructure is white. The U.S. fleet of ice breakers is home ported in Seattle so an Alaskan cruise can catch a glimpse of them

USCGC Healy is America's newest ice breaker. Built in 1999, it is the first American surface ship to reach the North Pole unaccompanied by another vessel. Photo by United States Geological Service.

there. Other countries use different colors for icebreakers but the hull shape makes it easy to identify them.

A relic of days gone by light ships can only be seen at maritime museums. The last U.S. light ship was decommissioned in 1985. It was boring duty for the men who operated these ships anchored in place.

Cutters interdict smugglers, protect U.S. interests throughout its Exclusive Economic Zone (out to 200 miles from shore), and conducts search and rescue missions. Painted white with a striking diagonal red blaze and smaller blue line down the hull near the bow, they are easy to recognize. Many of the coast guard

services of other nations use a similar color scheme.

Docked in Honolulu near the clock tower, you'll see a Coast Guard buoy tender. It is a smaller ship with an open deck and a crane to lift buoys out of the water. Other ports have them, but they are not as visible as in Hawaii.

A Coast Guard cutter home ported in Honolulu. .

Built in Finland, the Sorokin is a class of four Russian icebreakers.

Container ships

There are about 5,000 container ships plying the world ocean. You can identify them by the stacks of 20 or 40-foot-long containers strapped

Container ships have taken over maritime shipping. The cost to handle cargo drops by some 90% when using containers.

to their deck. Older ships carry about 5,000 TEUs, which is the standard of measurement. Newer ones carry three times that number. TEUs are "twenty foot equivalent units." So although most of the containers are 40' long, the unit of measurement is equivalent to a 20' container.

When close you can see how the containers are strapped to the deck. As well strapped down as they are, containers do fall overboard. Companies don't eagerly report when they lose a container so the

numbers are impossible to verify. The range of estimates is from about 2,500 a year to 10,000 a year.

Did you see the 2013 movie starring Robert Redford *All is Lost*? It is the tale of a single-handed sailor hitting a shipping container in the Indian Ocean. Watch it when you get back home. Such collisions do occur, but are rare.

Note how high a container ship is riding. Coming out of a Chinese port the black "boot topping" part of the hull may be barely visible. Going into a Chinese port, although stacked high with containers, ships typically ride high so you can see the "boot

Giant cranes load 40' containers onto a ship. Watch the industrial ballet as trucks deliver or take away containers as fast as each crane loads or unloads them. Thousands of containers can be off-loaded in just a few hours.

Giant machines re-arrange the stacks of containers in port. Ryan Bent Photography.

topping." Heading into China many of those containers are empty.

Container ships have accelerated the pace of global trade. 90% of the non-bulk cargoes are carried in container ships. By packing products inside containers and loading the containers, the ship's loading time has been greatly reduced as has stevedore pilferage.

Cruise ships

You can identify cruise ships easily. Most have enormous structure above the water line. This superstructure stretches from the stern almost to the bow. Most often it is painted white and has many portholes. At night cruise ships are lighted up both with deck lighting and cabin lights.

A cruise ship put to another purpose is the World Odyssey. During the fall and spring she hosts Semester at Sea. Over the summer she is renamed Deutschland and carries German passengers on European holidays. Photo by Ryan Bent.

Even professionals have bad days. This cruise ship went aground off Panama. No one was injured. Photo by Charles Ford.

Day shapes

Any ship that has limited abilities to maneuver should show an appropriate day shape signal. A commercial fishing boat should show two black cones. A vessel that

The Queen Mary 2 is flagship of the Cunard Line. Regal is her presence. Photo by Will Hayes.

is anchored should show a black ball. A barge or ship being towed will show a black diamond as will the tug that is towing it. Ships conducting surveys or research show a ball above a diamond above another ball.

The two black cones are the day shape used by fishing boats to tell other vessels that they have limited maneuvering ability.

When a ship is anchored it should raise a black ball to indicate it cannot maneuver.

Dredges

Transiting through a major canal will give you a glimpse of dredges. You can also see them in many ports. These can look like freighters with

huge pipes angling over their side. Some will have a pipeline extending back to the shore where the dredge spoils they dig up are deposited on land. Others may have a barge tied up to receive the dredged sediments from a scoop or bucket. When in operation they muddy the surrounding water.

Several dredges operate full-time in the Panama Canal. One dredge pumps spoils through a long set of pipes on-shore.

The Port of Kobe, Japan, uses this dredge to keep its harbor open to shipping.

Dry bulk carriers

For products that aren't liquids and are too low cost to pack in containers there are dry bulk carriers. Common products for these are cement, coal, logs, and grain. This sounds like the **Settlers of Catan** board game. Worldwide there about 17,000 dry bulk ships.

Most have open decks with several hatch covers. There can be several cranes on board, although some carry products that are sucked out with giant vacuums in port. If your travels take you to the port of Casa Blanca phosphate dust being loaded into bulk carriers will color the sky.

In port there will be holding tanks and loading/unloading apparatus. Grain or cement silos are easy to spot. Ports where logs are exported show large piles of logs, often with water sprinklers keeping them cool so they don't ignite.

If cargo is dry and is carried in containers it is dry bulk. Many of the world's commodities are carried in dry bulk carriers. You can identify them by the hatch covers on their deck. Many will have cranes to move the product on and off the ship. This ship is carrying logs and other products through the Kiel Canal. Photo by Rod Brown.

Not a semi-submersible, the Forte requires a crane to load and offload its cargo.

General cargo

There are some 10,000 cargo ships that are not containerized. They have cranes or gantry systems to load and unload cargo. Generally smaller than container ships they serve the smaller ports. Seeing several cranes or pairs of sticks is the clue that a ship is not a tanker.

General cargo ships are often smaller ships that can carry a variety of materials or products into smaller ports.

Heavy lift ships

There aren't many heavy lift ships, but they are interesting. They either require a giant crane to lift whatever they carry or they are semi-submersible, which means they take on water to lower the ship and float

The Mighty Servant 3 is a semi-submersible. It is loaded with part of an offshore oil rig waiting in port for several days of good weather. In 2010 she was refitted to help clean up the Deepwater Horizon oil disaster. Earlier in her career she sank while offloading an oil rig for Angola.

Hydrofoils get places quickly. Instead of displacing a large volume of water to move forward, they rise up out of the water on small foils. The reduced drag allows them to go fast. Vietnam uses a fleet of hydrofoils to move people.

the load off. They are used to carry oil product platforms to offshore sites.

Steel pipe is being off-loaded from this bulk carrier in Tromso, Norway.

Hydrofoils

Hydrofoils lift themselves out of the water so their weight is supported by underwater wings. Each wing connects to the hull on struts. Hydrofoils can achieve high speeds and fuel economies, but are expensive to build and maintain. They are used throughout the world in Hong Kong, Vietnam, the Baltic Sea, on the Danube, Japan, Korea, and Russia. The U.S. Navy had several hydrofoils in its fleet, but has retired them. Several other navies still use them.

These are easy to identify once they are up on their foils. They leave port looking like other boats. Once in the clear of other boats and the dock they rise up onto the foils and move quickly across the surface. And, they are noisy.

LNG carriers

These ships are easy to identify. Picture a tanker with three or more giant hemispheres on deck.

To get petroleum gas across the ocean it is cooled to minus 260 degrees F. As a liquid the gas (mostly

This ship carries liquid petroleum gas in the large cylinders seen rising above its deck. Most LNG carriers use very large spheres to carry the liquid natural gas.

methane) takes up 0.16% of the volume that it does as a gas.

On a ship the liquefied gas is stored in three to five giant metal spheres that take up the forward 80% of the ship. The spheres are the key to identifying these ships. However, some LNG carriers now have a covering over the spheres making it more difficult to ID them. The cover slopes upward and inward. On top of the cover is a maze of piping.

The bridge sits aft of the spheres and looks over them to navigate. There are about 1,800 of these ships in the world. Some carry LPG or liquefied petroleum gas (propane or butane) instead of LNG liquefied natural gas.

In port the LNG transfer station is removed from the other port facilities. If an LNG ship were to blow up, the force would be equivalent to several (some claim 50) atomic bombs. If there were ever a

"not in my backyard" industry, this would be it.

Naval vessels

Most navies have adopted a dark or haze gray color for their ships. Sometimes you'll see a lighter color tan or even camouflage.

Destroyers, cruisers, and similar classes all have a sharp bow and lean lines. They look fast. They have a central superstructure with lots of different shaped radar antenna on top. Most have rocket launchers which look like a package of hotdogs with square ends.

Comparing surface combatants from World War II and today reveals that the big guns are gone. They have been replaced by missile launchers. Most still have a single gun mounted forward, but not the multiple batteries of three huge guns.

Aircraft carriers are easy to identify: they are massive, most are over 1,000' long. The top of the conning tower is

An amphibious assault ship conducts training in Singapore Harbor. These large ships carry a contingent of marines and helicopters and landing craft to deliver the marines.

Instead of cannons modern destroyers carry rocket launchers. This is a Chinese destroyer.

200' above the water. The main deck is flat to accommodate launching and recovering aircraft. Some new designs have the flight deck angled upward to help launch planes. Since there are only a handful of aircraft carriers operating in the world (the US currently has 10), it's a special treat to see one. If your ship docks in San Diego you will see at least one, the USS Midway (a museum ship you can visit), and possibly two more at the Naval Base. If you land in Newport New, Virginia you're likely to see one, too. Several other countries have an aircraft carrier.

A now retired U.S. aircraft carrier, the USS Lake Champlain. The cost to build a new aircraft carrier is about $3 billion dollars and that doesn't include the airplanes. Photo by Charles Ford.

In addition to the traditional aircraft carrier there are somewhat shorter helicopter carriers and amphibious assault ships that have long flight decks. Seeing helicopters and vertical take-off airplanes on deck suggests a sighting is one of these smaller versions of an aircraft carrier.

Pilot boat

They deliver the pilot to the ship to guide it safely into port. And, they pick up the pilot after he has done his job and the ship is safely back out to sea. Many have the word "PILOT" plainly visible. They also show the "Hotel" or pilot aboard flag from their mast. This signal flag is divided into two vertical bands, one red and the other white.

Pilot boats bring pilots out to ships so the pilot can guide the ship into port. Leaving a port the pilot usually steps aboard while the ship is tied up and gets off onto a pilot boat once the ship has cleared the harbor or river.

Research ships

These tend to be smaller ships. Most have a large open deck on the stern with an A-frame crane and

The name Atlantis is fabled among the ocean research community. Atlantis 1 was a sailing ship. This is Atlantis 2 or A2. She has conducted research all over the world from her home in Woods Hole, Massachusetts. Photo by NASA.

There are many ships that carry cars and other equipment that roll on and roll off. Car carriers are big, bulky ships, usually painted white and having few portholes or windows.

several winches. If they are actively conducting a survey or have gear over the side they will show a "day shape" signal of a ball, over a diamond, over a ball. The day shapes are black. This "ball-diamond-ball" means the vessel has restricted maneuvering ability and that other ships should avoid coming near it.

Ro-Ro ships

Roll on, roll off ships handle cargo that can move itself or be towed aboard. This includes bulldozers, trucks, cranes, and cars. Many ro-ro ships have a massive stern door that folds down to make a ramp for vehicles and cargo to be moved on and off.

Car carriers are ro-ro, but the vertical clearance between decks is small so many levels of cars can be loaded. Ports that handle car imports or exports will have a steady stream of car carriers and large parking lots. Car carriers are very tall ships with a stout appearance. Nothing subtle or attractive about them. Vertical

Submarines are meant not to be seen so most often a sighting will occur in port.

This ferry serves Scotland and the Orkneys and Shetland Islands. Cars and trucks roll on and off and passengers can walk on or ride.

Truck trailers are hauled aboard this ro-ro ship in Scotland. Photo by Barbara Sobey.

sides, usually painted white, with no windows or portholes. If your ship berths near one watch the frantic movement of drivers as they race to get the cars on board.

The fancy new cars go to first world countries, but the ships don't have to go home empty. Often used cars are loaded aboard for sale in less wealthy countries.

Sailboats

Wherever you travel at sea you can find a hearty crew manning a sailboat. When you spot one the first thing you'll notice is the motion of the boat compared to whatever you are on. Sailboats rock and roll, but on many days provide an ideal passage with no engine noise and in tune with the sea.

There are many different types of sailing vessels. We'll mention the few that you are most likely to see.

The forward sail on this boat has been furled, and the mainsail has been reefed (shortened) due to high winds.

Some sailing ships will have square sails. Most have fore and aft sails. To identify the type, note first the number of masts. Most have one mast and are "sloop rigged." There is one sail in front of the mast that can be a jib, genoa, or spinnaker for down-wind sailing. The sail aft of the mast is the mainsail.

If the boat has two masts, notice which mast is taller. Usually the first mast will be taller, and the boat will be either a ketch or yawl. It can be difficult to differentiate between

Ketches and yawls each have two masts with the forward mast being the taller.

We sailed a 54' ketch from Yokosuka to Seattle years ago. Storm after storm battered us as we crossed first to Adak, Alaska and then down to Seattle. It was a grand adventure that took six weeks.

the two classes, but the second or mizzen mast on a ketch is in front of the rudder post. It is significantly in front of the back of the boat and the sail it carries, the mizzen sail, is good sized. On a yawl, the mast is nearly at the end of the boat and the sail it carries is much smaller.

Schooners have two masts with the second one taller. Schooners can have more than two masts but they are very rare. Photo by Peter Van Demark.

With two masts if the second mast is taller the boat is a schooner. Notice if the top of the sails is supported by a gaff or boom. This would make it a gaff-headed schooner. If you're keeping score of your observations you get extra credit for spotting one of these.

Tankers

There are about 12,000 tankers. 7,000 carry crude oil and the rest carry either refined petroleum products or other chemicals. When fully loaded they lie very low in the water. When empty of cargo, the hull sits very high. So high you can sometimes see the propeller and rudder.

Decks are covered with a maze of pipes. The superstructures, where the bridge and crew cabins are, sit near the stern of the ship. Often some warning is written on the front of the superstructure such as "No smoking."

Before the Exxon Valdez disaster in 1989 tankers operating in U.S. waters were single hull. So, if they ran aground as the Exxon Valdez did, a breach in the hull meant a significant spillage of oil. Now tankers are required to be double-hulled so a breach in the outer hull won't lead to a spill. A high-speed collision, however, could breach both hulls.

Tankers will not dock anywhere near cruise ship terminals. Ports have a separate dock with on-land storage tanks.

Giant oil tankers ply the seas full of oil in one direction and riding much higher in the other direction. Smaller tankers carry refined products and chemicals often to smaller ports.

What fun it is to be greeted by a fireboat when entering a Japanese port. It doesn't happen every time, but have your camera ready.

How to identify a ship

If you can see the name of the ship you can find it on the internet. Unique names may pop up from a general search. For a specific search in your area use a vessel identification service like www.marinetraffic.com. This site allows you to search for ships in your area or to look up names of ships.

You can find the name of a ship by locating the ship you are on and

You can see floating dry docks in many ports. Like submarines they take on water, so they sink far enough for a ship to move into them. Divers place blocks beneath them holding the ship in place. Then the water is pumped out raising the dock with ship. Now workers can repair and paint the hull.

seeing what ships are nearby. Again, go to marinetraffic.com and search for your ship. They have a map that will show the position of the ship you searching for. The map will show all the vessels within range. When you find the other ship, click on it to reveal its name, destination, and other information.

This system of ship identification is called the Automatic Identification System. Ships communicate their position, speed, destination port, and recent itinerary to stations on shore and to satellites. By clicking on the ship on the map you open pages that show ownership, construction details, and more.

Naval vessels and some others will switch off their identification system for security. Another use for this service is seeing where your ship is so you can find it for embarkation. Or, to find out what other ships are in or will be coming into port.

Chapter 6

Energy at Sea:
Fish, Oil, and Power

ENERGY IS INCREASINGLY BEING HARVESTED FROM the sea or at sea. Marine wind farms are common in English and European waters. Some wind farms contain hundreds of turbines. Oil exploration and production platforms can be seen in the Gulf of Mexico, Persian Gulf, and the North Sea. Almost anywhere you go you'll find fishing.

Oil drilling rigs and production platforms are seen throughout the Gulf of Mexico, North Sea, and the Baltic Sea, and off Brazil, Trinidad, West Africa, Southeast Asia, Alaska,

Large floating platforms like this one can be towed to the lease site. There the platforms take in ballast water to increase their stability. Moorings hold them in position while they drill for oil.

This is part of the London Array or wind farm just off the Thames estuary. With 175 wind turbines, it is the largest offshore wind farm. Other large wind farms are located in the North and Baltic Seas.

Venezuela and other countries. Cruise ships will stay away from these structures, but you might see them at sea or in ports (such as Stavanger, Norway). Some oil production platforms burn the natural gas that they find with the oil. This makes a spectacular scene from miles away at night.

Once offloaded from the heavy transport ship, the three giant legs are pushed downward to the bottom to support the platform. This is a jack-up rig.

These giant structures are oil rigs. They are stored in port until they are needed by an oil company. These are in Norway.

Gathering fish

Fishing is the most ancient way of harvesting energy at sea. And, it is changing throughout the world. Fish stocks are down in many of the major fisheries and aquaculture is replacing it. Both traditional fishing and fish farming are visible from the deck of a ship.

Fishing boats and fishers and can be found anywhere in the world. Wild fish are disappearing from the seas and are being replaced by

This Costa Rican fishing boat is a purse seiner. It surrounds a school of fish with a net. The small boat at the back of the fishing boat drags the end of the net around and back to the fishing boat. Like the drawstrings on a purse, lines are pulled taut to create a net bag that is then hauled aboard. If a fishing boat carries a small boat on its deck, it is likely to be a purse seiner.

This is a Russian fishing trawler in the Port of Tromso, Norway. The ramp at the stern is how nets full of fish are winched aboard this boat.

farmed fish. But there are still many thousands of fishing boats out on the ocean.

Fishing is done in several different ways. Fishermen use throw nets in shallow water or from a small boat to capture small fish. These can be either eaten or used as bait for fishing with hook and line. In Cochin, India instead of using throw nets they have

Fishermen are working on their nets as a swarm of anxious sea gulls circle overhead. Photo by Will Hayes.

Made famous by its multiple appearances in the television show America's Deadliest Catch, the Early Dawn is tied up in Dutch Harbor, Alaska. She is a crabber. Aboard is Captain Rick Fehst. Photo by Rick Fehst.

giant teeter-totters with a net on one end. Workers pull on the other end of the long lever arm to lift the net and fish out of the bay.

Fish traps are used almost everywhere. In their simplest form a row of sticks or rocks blocks the

Traveling the world by cruise ship exposes you to traditional fishing practices. Here the fisherman is using a throw net. The weights pull the net towards the bottom and a draw line closes the net around the fish. The fisherman dumps his catch into his small boat. Photo by Bill Yeaton.

Two Indian fishermen maneuver their canoe with a one-handed paddle. To move farther they use oars. Photo by Bill Yeaton.

Fish traps are a common site throughout the world. A line of sticks supports a net. Fish swimming parallel to shore are guided into a pocket. Although some fish escape the pocket, many don't find the opening. At low tide the owner uses a small net to retrieve fish caught in the pocket. This fish trap is on the island of Rangiroa, French Polynesia. Photo by Bill Yeaton.

passage of fish along the shore and directs them into a trap. Fishermen harvest the trap at low tide by dip netting or just hand catching the fish in the trap. As you look along the shore notice any regular arrangement of vertical wooden sticks.

Circular rings support netting that holds thousands of salmon of cod. Fishermen catch smaller fish to feed them or use the waste from fish processing factories. Increasingly fish food is created from on-land crops.

Fish farming is conducted in a variety of ways. Salmon and other high value fish are reared in large net cages in bays where there is good water circulation. The tipoff that you're looking at a fish farm are rows of circular structures floating on the water. They are common in the fjords of Norway and Chile, and along the coast of British Columbia and many other places.

Shellfish aquaculture doesn't require net cages; rope hangs down from floats with the shellfish attached to the rope. The visual give-away is the regularly spaced floats near shore. Often a shack is mounted on a float that is adjacent to the farm.

These floats support lines on which muscles grow. The muscles filter feed to eat so muscle farms need to be located in protected areas that have good water flow.

This boat carries live fish from fish farms to processing or between fish farms. This is the Martin Seale.

To protect the interests and fishing laws requires a fishery enforcement vessel. Here is the Jura in the Shetland Islands. Scotland has three enforcement ships plus two aircraft.

Chapter 7

What Else Can You See?

EVEN IF WHALES ARE TAKING THE DAY OFF AND no pelagic birds are in sight, there are many phenomena to notice. Some are visual, but as you already know, some assault all your other senses too.

As your ship or boat moves through the water you know instinctively what the weather conditions are. If the bow is rising and falling, you are heading into rough seas. If you are rocking noticeably from side to side, waves are hitting the ship on the beam. Walking onto the deck provides lots more information if you can decipher it.

Wind patterns

Sea breeze and land breeze

Close to shore the wind can change direction twice daily. In the early morning you will see the breeze is from the land toward the sea. This is a "land breeze." Winds, unlike ocean currents, are described by the direction the air comes from, not the direction it is traveling. So a land breeze moves toward the ocean.

Overnight, especially if the night sky was cloud-free, the land surface cools. It cools the air above it making the air denser. The air above the ocean does not cool off at night or heat up as much during the day due to the greater heat capacity of water. With denser air over land and less dense air over the sea, the denser air pushes the lighter sea air out of the way.

During the day as the land heats up and it heats the air above it, this air becomes less dense and rises. Again the temperature of the water doesn't change as quickly as the temperature on land, so the air above the ocean doesn't change much during one day. Air from over the ocean is now denser and flows on-shore creating a sea breeze.

Watch the direction flags are blowing when in port. You may see them switch directions throughout the day. However any storms or strong wind systems will interrupt this land breeze/sea breeze cycle. The land/sea breeze phenomena extends only a few miles out to sea.

Trade winds and westerlies

You can witness the planet's dominant wind patterns on oceanic voyages. Heading north or south you might pass from one climatic regime to the next. One morning the winds are from the west and the next morning they are blowing from the east.

Such a change in wind direction doesn't guarantee you're in a new regime. Storms passing can shift the winds over a few hours. But if the winds persist from the new direction you are likely to have changed regimes.

Most people live in subtropical or temperate climates. These climates prevail from the tropics to the polar circles. Looking at a world map the temperate region extends from 23.5 degrees latitude to 66.5 degrees. Of course you won't see a radical change crossing over these lines. But

One of several proposed origins for the term "horse latitudes" is that Spanish ships becalmed in these regions of light wind would run out of water. With not enough water to keep crew alive, they wouldn't share any with livestock aboard so they would push any horses into the sea.

traveling at 20 knots for a day can take you from predominately western winds of the temperate region into the trade winds blowing from the east.

Atmospheric high pressure regions predominate from about 30 – 38 degrees latitude. Poleward of these regions winds are westerly (meaning they come from the west). On the equatorial side of these regions the winds are easterly. Between the two regions are the "horse latitudes" where the winds can be light and variable. If storms don't interrupt these average wind patterns, you can see the change in predominant winds over a few days' time sailing northward or southward through these regions.

At latitudes higher than the horse latitudes, winds and weather predominately come from the west. Conditions are dominated by periods of storms and periods of fair weather. Watching the ships barometer or seeing the atmospheric pressure on the weather report will tell you what to expect. Rising atmospheric pressure indicates improving weather. A falling barometer suggests stormy weather. Rapidly falling suggests a rapidly approaching storm.

As you sail from the horse latitudes towards the equator the wind regime changes. The winds are predominately from the northeast in the northern hemisphere and southeast in the southern hemisphere. The wind direction is consistent. The strength of the winds varies typically increasing during the day and dropping overnight.

Tropical islands are constantly bathed by the trade winds. Islanders won't use compass directions to indicate where a place is located. Instead they will describe it as being on either the windward or leeward side of their island. The side of the island facing into the wind will be noticeably wetter than the leeward side only a few miles away. On the big island of Hawaii the windward side, Hilo, gets 127 inches of rain a year. Kona, on the leeward side, gets one tenth of that amount. As the trade winds come onshore the humid ocean air is lifted up by the topography of the islands. The moisture in the air condenses, and rain occurs. On the leeward side, the now drier air, rides down the topography leaving clear skies.

Intertropical Convergence Zone

The trade winds end at the meteorological equator, which is called the Intertropical Convergence Zone (ITCZ). With the most intense solar heating of the ocean, the air above it is warm and laden with evaporated water. Water vapor rises creating a belt of clouds that show up in satellite views of earth. This is the doldrums.

The ITCZ moves seasonally north and south, but generally is within 5 degrees of the geographic equator. Winds are very light and sailing vessels can have difficulties crossing the doldrums. If you're sailing through them you'll notice the seas are often flat. They are even glassy sometimes. You may see a gentle

The intertropical convergence zone shows up in NASA photos as a band of clouds roughly at the geographic equator.

swell from some storm thousands of miles away, but the seas are quite calm. As you continue poleward through the doldrums you will awake one morning to find yourself in the trade winds again. But now you will note that although the winds are still from the east, they are now from the southeast if you're in the southern hemisphere or the northeast if you're in the northern hemisphere.

Tropic of Cancer and Tropic of Capricorn

The tropics of Cancer and Capricorn lie at latitudes of 23.5. The Tropic of Cancer being in the northern hemisphere with Capricorn in the southern hemisphere. What an odd place to put two major geographic lines! Note, too, that the Arctic Circle and Antarctic Circle lie at latitudes 66.5 degrees. What gives, you might ask?

Early in earth's history it collided with its future moon. The collision with a large space rock called "Theia" occurred about 4.5 billion years ago, just 100 million years after the earth formed. We think the debris created by this collision coalesced into the moon, which continues to move slowly away from earth.

The second result of the collision is that the earth doesn't rotate around an axis perpendicular to its orbit around the sun. The earth spins 23.5 degrees off vertical. That's why we have annual seasons. When the northern hemisphere tilts towards the sun, it receives more solar radiation and it's summer. Since summer also brings a smaller difference in solar heating between the equator and the North Pole, storms in summer are weaker. Storms depend on differences in temperature. The bigger the difference, the more frequent and stronger the storms are.

Summer gives us higher temperatures and weaker storms. For the northern hemisphere this occurs when the earth is farthest from the sun, in early January. It turns out that the earth's distance to the sun has less impact on seasons than does the tilt caused by the collision with Theia.

The earth doesn't revolve around the sun in a circle. It travels in an ellipse, hence its distance to the sun varies throughout the year. And, its speed of travel changes throughout the year. It's moving slower in June, July, and August so the Northern Hemisphere enjoys four more days of summer than does the Southern Hemisphere.

How far was the earth's axis knocked off vertical by that collision with Theia? 23.5 degrees. The polar circles (at 90 minus 23.5 degrees latitude or 66.5 degrees) mark the limits of 24-hour sunshine on the summer solstice and 24-hour darkness on the winter solstice. The Tropics of Cancer and Capricorn are located where the sun is overhead on the first day of summer in each hemisphere.

Hurricanes

In the tropics you can bet on the consistent winds. Exceptions occur, especially in hurricane season. Hurricanes generally form in the east side of oceans and migrate west in the same direction as the trade winds. The northern hemisphere hurricane season is June 1 through November 30. In the Indian Ocean it begins earlier and ends later. In the southern hemisphere Pacific and Indian Oceans the season is October through May.

As a quirk of geography, the South Atlantic Ocean is all but hurricane free. Look at a chart of hurricane paths to see many hurricane tracks streaking across the other oceans, but almost none in the South Atlantic.

Hurricanes are huge storms that draw heat and water vapor from the sea and transform them into intense winds and rain. This is a NASA GEOS satellite image of Hurricane Irene in 2011.

Be assured the navigation team is well informed on tropical storms and their anticipated path and will move out of their way whenever possible. Most cruise companies employ multiple weather prediction companies to advise them on approaching storms and on optimal routing to avoid rough weather.

Sailing from Honolulu to Tokyo we ducked farther south to avoid a string of strong storms in the western Pacific. We crossed the Pacific Ocean below the tracks of these temperate region storms, but eventually had to come north to reach Tokyo. Then for a day and a half the ship rocked and rolled, and we passed out seasick bags. As rough as the last few days were, that route was a much better than sailing directly across the Pacific through the string of storms.

Hurricanes, typhoons, and tropical cyclones are all the same. They have winds greater than 63 knots and originate in the tropics or subtropics. They need the moisture evaporated from the ocean to power their strong winds. In the Atlantic and Northeast Pacific they are called hurricanes. In the western North Pacific they are called typhoons and in the South Pacific Ocean and Indian Ocean there are called cyclones. Different names for the same weather phenomena.

Predict the weather

The most dependable way to know what the weather will be is to log onto a weather site. Most sites do not provide weather forecasts for the oceans. However, there are several sites that do. PassageWeather.com is a good one. It will show you predicted winds, waves, and rain for several days for most marine areas.

Eschewing the internet and using your observational skills, the most reliable predictions for later are based on what is happening now. What you see is likely what you will get in the short term. When conditions are going to change you can see the change signals coming.

These high clouds can indicate that a storm is approaching. If lower clouds follow them by 12 -24 hours, a storm is approaching.

From the deck you can see storms coming 24 to 48 hours before they hit. One indication is the growth of swell. If a storm is creating swell the ship will roll or pitch more. At first the swell will be mild and the distance between successive wave crests will be large. As you get closer to the storm the swell build and shorten. That is, as the storm approaches the swell crests will get close together and steeper.

In the sky change is often indicated first by the growth of the highest fleecy clouds, the cirrus. These are ice clouds and indicate that there is moisture in the high atmosphere. Often you will see them and a few hours later they will dissipate suggesting no change in the weather. But if the cirrus clouds are followed by lower stratus clouds – sheets of clouds – weather is approaching.

The white puffy cotton ball clouds called cumulus clouds are often a sign of fair weather. If they have flat bottoms, the air is stable, and the clouds are not likely to grow vertically into a local storm. These clouds represent water that has been evaporated from the sea. Directly beneath them air currents are upward, from sea to cloud. At their edges air currents are downward, forming a convection cell. Warm, moist air rises and condenses into water vapor that you see as clouds.

Notice the edge of the clouds. They are constantly changing. The water vapor is evaporating and disappearing or condensing and emerging.

If the bottom of the clouds is rough, the air is unstable. Rising air might tend to keep rising in the atmosphere. Watch throughout the day to see if the cumulus clouds grow taller. They can grow into thunderstorms usually by late afternoon. Yes, thunderstorms with lightning do occur at sea.

How strong is the wind?

You can find the current weather conditions on most ship's home channel available on the television in your cabin. This probably comes from a thermometer, barometer, hygrometer, and an anemometer spinning wildly above the bridge. Whatever the anemometer measures has to be adjusted to account for the ship's motion. A 20 knot (kts) headwind combined with a ship's speed of 20 kts makes a 40 kts apparent wind. This makes a turn

Wind speeds above 15 or 16 knots cause whitecaps to form. This is a good indicator of wind speed at sea. Photo by Barbara Sobey.

around the deck unpleasant. A 20 kt tail wind with the same ship's speed

Beaufort scale

Beaufort Number	Condition	Wind Speed (knots)	Description
0	Calm	Less than 1	Sea surface is flat
1	Light air	1-3	Small ripples appear
2	Light breeze	4-6	Small waves with glassy crests
3	Gentle breeze	7-10	Larger waves; some breaking
4	Moderate breeze	11-16	More frequent waves breaking, whitecaps
5	Fresh breeze	17-21	White caps everywhere; some spray
6	Strong breeze	22-27	Lots of spray off tops of waves
7	Near gale	28-33	Spindrift forms from top of waves
8	Gale	34-40	Moderate sized waves; foam blown into streaks
9	Strong gale	41-47	Large waves. Difficult to see due to spray.
10	Storm	48-55	Very high waves. Entire sea covering in white foam.
11	Violent storm	56-63	Exceptionally high waves. Visibility is difficult due to spray.
12	Hurricane	Higher than 63	Worse than 11

and direction makes for an almost wind free walk.

Before anemometers were invented sailors estimated the wind speed by looking at the sea. Since waves are a product of the wind, looking at the waves gives you a good idea of how strong the wind is. There are a couple of caveats, however.

Wave height depends on wind speed, how long the wind has been blowing at that speed and direction, and the distance over the ocean the wind has been blowing. A sudden breeze regardless of how strong it is will not raise great waves. But sustain that wind for a few hours over 100 miles (fetch) and the waves get huge.

The idea of estimating wind speed by observing waves came from British admiral Francis Beaufort. The noon report from the bridge may include the current sea state on the Beaufort scale.

The Beaufort scale

The Beaufort scale categorizes sea state in 12 descriptions. Each sea state has a range of winds associated with it.

If the sea surface is glassy smooth (don't we wish!) the wind speed is zero. This condition does occur and more often than you might think. In a boat powered by sails this can be an eerie experience in the middle of an ocean.

If you can see small ripples on the surface, but no breaking waves the wind is 1-3 knots. At these low speeds you might see "cats' paws" or riffled patches of water dance across the water, responding to gusts of wind.

When a flag on a stationary pole extends, the wind is up to at least 7 knots. At lower wind speeds flag motion is desultory.

A major change in the appearance of the sea surface occurs at 15 – 16 knots of wind. Whitecaps form everywhere. There might be some ambiguity about changes from one sea state to another, but the appearance of whitecaps is impossible to miss.

When spray blows off the top of the whitecaps the wind is 17 knots or higher. Around 25 knots you'll hear wires above you whistle. The wind moving over and under the wires swirls into eddies. As the wire vibrates back and forth, it sheds the eddies and produces the whistling sound.

At 30 knots winds knock water off the tops of waves into streaks. Spindrift blows off the tops of waves and the sea looks confused. You're in a gale and this would be a good time to get off the deck and watch from inside. Higher wind speeds continue to build the waves and make energetic streaks across the surface.

There are variations of the Beaufort scale for wind observations on land. Watching how trees respond to different wind speeds provides the information you get at sea by looking at the water surface. You can find a complete table on line or in the ship's library. Above is an abbreviated table.

Of course there are hurricanes and there are bigger hurricanes. Hurricanes have their own scale called the Saffir-Simpson Hurricane Wind Scale. This scale is not based on observations of the water surface as the Beaufort scale is. At hurricane wind speeds it's difficult to see the surface. So, it is based entirely on wind speed. Level 1 starts at 64 knots. The highest level, 5, is above 113 knots.

Why we use knots?

Announcements of ship's and wind speed will be given in knots or nautical miles per hour. Knots per hour sometimes is uttered, but only by those who don't know that knots is a speed not a distance. The measure of distance at sea is the nautical mile. The measure of speed is knots.

It might seem crazy to have specific units for distance (nautical mile) and speed (knots) at sea when we are used to different measures of speed and distance on land. But

The line starts here. The prime meridian is marked by the line in the ground, emanating from inside the walls of the Greenwich Observatory.

The Greenwich Observatory, on the Thames River in England, is the center of the earth. Through this location runs the prime meridian or the 00 line of longitude. The line is marked in the Observatory.

the nautical units are based on geography and logic. Not so the statute mile. A nautical mile is one "minute of latitude." One minute of latitude is 1/60th of a degree, with 360 degrees around the globe. Thus the nautical mile (6,076') is based on the circumference of the earth. Makes sense. It especially makes sense if you are plotting a ship's course on a chart that uses latitude and longitude.

The convenience is that a navigator can easily measure distance on a chart in nautical miles. He sets his dividers according to the latitude printed on the side of the chart and "steps off" the distance between two points by swinging the dividers on a line between the points. Voila, he has the distance in nautical miles.

Compare the logic and utility of the nautical mile to a statute mile (5,280'). The statute mile is the distance unit many of us use on land. It is based on the length of a furrow a farmer could plow with a team of oxen. The standard unit of measurement in England in the 16th century was the furlong (220 yards) or the length of a furrow. A furrow is the distance a farmer could plow before resting the oxen. An acre is based on this odd measurement, too. An acre is one furlong in length and one chain (66') in width. Queen Elizabeth picked eight of these furlongs to be the English measure for a mile (5,280') so it would be close to the Roman mile (5,000'). So the statute mile is based on how far oxen could plow fields in England in the 16th century and has not much value except for confusing people who are used to the more user friendly metric system.

Not to be outdone by the English, the French invented their own mile that we call the kilometer. It is 3,280' long. From a geographer's perspective it has much more logic behind it than the distance farmers could plow their fields. A kilometer is 1,000 meters and a meter is one ten millionth of the distance from the equator to the North Pole. The formal definition specifies that the line has to pass through Paris. So there you Englishmen!

The meter has been re-defined several times. The most recent definition is based on the speed of light. One meter is the distance light travels through a vacuum in 1/299,792,458 of a second.

The English of course defined the global positioning grid so the zero line of longitude, the zero meridian, passes through the Royal Observatory in Greenwich.

Where do the waves come from?

Even on calm days at sea there are low waves undulating across the surface. Most of the time the sea surface is a riot of wave energy, some generated locally and some from

Why are nautical miles per hour called "knots?" Before GPS and mechanical knot meters, sailors measured a ship's speed with a rope. They tossed one end of a rope overboard. At the end of the rope was a wood panel that dragged it through the water to pull the coiled rope behind it. A sailor would count the number of evenly-spaced knots in the line that were pulled overboard for 30 seconds. The timing being provided by a sand-glass timer. The speed, which was the number of knots, was recorded and used by the navigator to estimate how far the ship had traveled along its current heading.

hundreds if not thousands of miles away.

Waves are generated by winds. As the winds blow along the surface they create capillary waves. These waves are tiny and the dominant force pulling them back to a smooth surface is the surface tension of water. Spreading oil on the water to reduce surface tension and capillary waves was one prescription to calm the waters in a storm.

Once wind causes capillary waves to form, waves can grow quickly. The tiny undulations give the wind a surface to push against. The transfer of energy from wind to water is more effective after capillary waves form.

Surface tension is so strong at small scales that it allows you to "float" steel on water. Try this with a paper clip in a cup of water. The trick to doing this is don't let your fingers touch the water. Use a second paperclip bent as a tool to lower the first one gently on the surface. With some care you can get the paperclip to float on the surface. The surface tension that holds the paperclip comes from molecules of water sticking to each other. Touching the water or adding a drop of soap will reduce the surface tension, letting the paperclip fall.

The larger waves are "gravity waves" as gravity and not surface tension is the dominant force opposing their formation. If the wind direction is steady, the waves keep growing. But, of course in a storm the wind direction and speed change within hours. Thus the sea surface becomes a visual cacophony of water crashing into water and waves overtaking other waves.

Waves travel on the sea surface with little loss of energy. Although the individual crest you see doesn't travel far, the set of waves does. The wave crest in front dies and a new one forms behind. The waves crashing on the beach in Hawaii could have been generated by a storm in the Gulf of Alaska or the in Southern Hemisphere.

Watching the waves from the deck of your ship you can differentiate the waves generated locally from those created far away. Once generated waves move across the ocean. They merge with other waves and get longer and more organized. The distance from one crest to the next increases. These can be the gentle swell that rock you to sleep or the annoying 15 second waves that keep you off balance.

Waves created near you have shorter wave lengths and are not as organized. They slam into the ship at less predictable intervals. It is these

Feeling a bit of Neptune's disease? The patches seem to help. Before the waves get big, cut one in half to see if half is enough to ease your mal der mer. Also stay near a window and look at the horizon. Some people swear by the wrist bands. Hopefully you will quickly adjust to the motion.

Try timing how long it takes your ship or boat to roll with the waves. Each vessel has its natural rolling rate that depends on its size and design. Typical for ocean cruise ships is 13 seconds. Giant ships will roll at a slower rate. In a 60' boat the rocking is much faster.

waves that are responsible for the queasy feeling in your stomach.

Waves from near and far

Winds generate waves, but not all the waves you see are generated by the winds you feel. Waves can travel long distances. Some will travel across an ocean. A storm off of Japan can send its wave crashing into San Diego.

Looking out over the ocean you might notice that there well developed waves that have several seconds between wave crests as well as the less organized waves created by the winds that you feel. The long, organized waves are "swell." They started life as shorter, disorganized waves called "sea."

As sea waves move away from the winds that created them, they organize into the faster-moving waves. These rock your ship gently (usually). On top of the swell are the sea waves created by the winds you feel on your face.

Since there could be several storms in an ocean at any time, the swell you see could be coming from different directions. Can you sort out the sea surface? Can you see what directions the swell are coming from?

How big are those waves?

It's hard to tell. Standing on the top deck you may be 100' above the water surface, which makes it difficult to judge height. Equally difficult is standing in a small boat with your feet nearly at sea level and looking up at the waves.

If you're sailing on a commercial cruise ship, listen to the captain's daily report at noon for his estimate and compare it to your own. His is always higher than mine.

Wave height is measured from the top of the crest to the bottom of the trough. When the seas are calm with just a gentle swell, estimating wave height isn't too difficult. But as the seas get choppy or rough, estimating height is very difficult. In a confused sea waves come from two or three directions, all interfering with each other.

Try following the crest of one wave as it approaches your vessel. In front of your eyes it merges with others or disappears. Only distinct swell from far away are easy to track.

The tallest wave ever recorded was in 1933. The USS Ramapo, an oiler and survey ship, was crossing the Pacific Ocean when it experience a rogue wave 112' high. In 2016 a 62' tall rogue wave set the world record for the largest wave recorded by instrumentation. For more about rogue waves, see the section below.

Will we see a rogue wave?

No. Or, more accurately you are very unlikely to experience one. Ships will try to avoid serious storms where rogues are more common. Cruise companies want happy customers, not people green with motion sickness. For small boats avoiding storms is even more important and everyone pays attention to weather forecasts.

Rogue waves are ephemeral – they last for a few seconds and are gone. They won't chase you across the ocean. One develops and quickly dies.

Rogue waves are not magical. They arise from normal wind waves that run into each other. Waves travel at different speeds. Longer waves travel faster and overtake shorter waves. As two or more waves merge, their crests can coincide to give a height higher than either of the parent waves. To officially be a rogue, a wave must be twice the average height of the highest surrounding waves. This doesn't happen often.

Tsunami?

Tsunamis or tidal waves arise from earthquakes, volcanic eruptions, and underwater landslides. The sudden movement of huge amounts of earth's material can, but doesn't always, trigger a wave or a series of waves. Tsunamis move at incredible speeds across an ocean, up to 500 mph. Imagine one slamming into your ship!

You won't feel it. The height of a tsunami at sea is about 3 feet. That height is spread out over a wavelength (distance from crest to crest) of maybe 200 miles. The wave hitting your ship will lift your ship 3' over the course of a half hour. You won't notice it. The wave will zip by you and be gone and no one will have seen it.

This tsunami warning siren is on the Hawaiian Island of Molokai. Similar sirens can be found in coastal areas of many countries.

On shore, however, the tsunami can be destructive. As the 200 mile long wave moves into shallow coastal water it does what all waves do. It slows down. The front slows down first so the back catches up. The wavelength decreases and the wave height increases. If the wave energy is funneled into a bay, the wave height can be enormous. In 1958, a tsunami generated a wave 1,700' high in Lituya Bay, Alaska. Not as tall but much more deadly was the 2006 tsunami in the Indian Ocean that killed 230,000 people.

With seismic stations around the world looking for earthquakes, you're likely to have a warning that a tsunami might occur. The predictions are alerts to the possibility, not to the existence of a tsunami. At many places around the world you will see large sirens mounted on poles along the coast and signs mounted giving directions of where to go if the siren sounds. Had these existed in Indonesia in 2006 thousands of lives would have been saved.

Absent warning of any kind, if your walk along a remote beach shows a rapidly decreasing sea level, don't pursue it seaward. Move to high ground. Even moving a few hundred yards inland could save your life. Before the crest of the tsunami wave hits, the trough arrives and sea level falls. You now have minutes to get to a safe location.

The Monterey Bay Aquarium's Seafood Watch is an excellent place to get scientific information on the sustainability of fisheries and on making healthy choices in eating seafood.

Where is the garbage patch?

You've heard about a mountain of trash in the middle of the Pacific Ocean. Will you see it?

It's unlikely that you'll see a mound of garbage, but occasionally you can. The greatest concentrations of trash are near the centers of each ocean – not just the Pacific. Most trans-oceanic voyages don't go through the centers. Sailing from the west coast to Hawaii ships skirt the edge of the eastern North Pacific patch, but that's as close as most cruises come.

What you do see on every cruise in every ocean is a steady stream of tiny bits of plastic. Many more bits of plastic than fish. It's everywhere.

Imagine a 26-ton dump truck pulling up to the ocean and dumping a load of plastic into the sea. Repeat that every 2 minutes 24 hours a day, 365 days a year. That's the volume that's entering the ocean.

Of course there are tons more of other material being dumped too. But much of this material degrades relatively quickly. The plastic can take years, decades, or longer.

What do you do with nets that aren't useful anymore? Too often the answer is cut them loose in the ocean and let them continue to catch and kill fish and mammals. Here a discarded net is being hauled aboard another fishing boat so it can be disposed of on land. Photo by Rick Fehst.

Big plastic pieces break down into many little pieces quickly. Walk along a beach anywhere in the world and sift through the stuff along the high tide line. You're find bits of plastic.

You can find the tiny remains of big pieces, pre-production nurdles, and micro-beads. Nurdles (5mm diameter spheres of HDPE) are sent to factories to be extruded into new plastic products. The U.S. produces 60 million pounds of these are year. Each pound has 25,000 nurdles, so when a bag breaks in shipment, thousands of nurdles go everywhere. They go right through sewage treatment systems into the ocean where they are perfectly sized and shaped to look like tasty fish eggs.

Smaller still are the micro plastic beads used in a variety of products including tooth paste and exfoliate scrubs. Some U.S. states have outlawed them and some manufacturers have agreed to phase

them out, but there are billions of them swirling around in the ocean.

Washing your favorite fleece jacket releases upwards of 250,000 synthetic fibers that swirl down the drain, through waste water treatment plants, and into the ocean. The ocean has been invaded by plastic.

The problem with plastic in the ocean is that it's long lived and it looks like food. As it floats near the surface it photo-oxidizes and then sinks, but stays in the surface waters. Organic pollutants adhere to the plastic pieces so when they are swallowed by fish, birds, or turtles the toxins go along. Large pieces, and rubber balloons, get caught in throats. Estimates for numbers of turtles and marine birds killed each year are staggering.

Plastic pre-production nurdles are buried along the high tide line on a beach. This beach is on one of the distant offshore islands off Belize. Photo by Kiera Ryan.

To complete this tale of woe, what are you having for dinner tonight? If seafood is on the menu think about the bio-accumulation of toxins in the food web. That salmon ate a hundred fish that each ate hundreds of smaller animals, each of which ate dozens of pieces of toxic plastic. Recommendations today are eat wild-caught ocean fish, but only once or twice a month. Check with your doctor and don't assume that all fish is healthy.

Most of the pollution in the ocean comes from land, but some comes from ships, oil platforms, and lost shipping containers. Estimates vary wildly about how many of the 40' containers are lost each year, but a safe estimate is more than 2,000 and less than 10,000. Stories abound of beach combers searching for a size 11 left foot Nike shoe to pair up with the right-footed shoe they found before. Or the thousands of rubber duckies that, dumped at sea in a storm, show up at beaches around the world. Or, Lego pieces by the thousands showing up on beaches in Europe.

Thousands of containers are lost at sea each year. Some are even lost in port. This container fell into the water in Accra, Ghana while being loaded onto a ship. It took hours to get divers into the water to rig lifting straps and then to get a crane to pick it up.

About to leave Accra, Ghana with Semester at Sea, we were standing on deck. The ship directly in front of us was loading shipping containers. Something happened and one was dropped into the water. An expensive mistake that raises the question of how often this happens.

To retrieve the container divers were called. They had to pass a lifting harness around the barely floating container. Then a crane was brought in to lift the container out of the water. The crew continued to struggle with the errant container as we sailed away.

Discarded fishing gear is another huge problem. When a net is no longer worth using, it is tossed overboard where it continues to catch fish, turtles, and marine mammals. The nets are made of nylon-like plastics that survive very nicely for many years in the ocean.

How to see the garbage patch

Look over the side as far forward as you can go. There is a patch of water near the ship not stirred up by the bow. Stare directly down and if the seas are not rough you will see a fleck of stuff passing every few seconds. Most of that is plastic. Some pieces will be on the surface, but many will be a few inches below the surface. You have to wonder how many more pieces are deeper, beyond your vision.

Concentrations of garbage in the patches is estimated to nearly 900,000 pieces in a square mile. And there are lots of square miles out there. Bigger than Texas? It's difficult and expensive to measure so we don't really have good estimates. Away from the garbage patches the concentration drops to 46,000 pieces per square mile. Only 46,000!

The hype is that islands of trash are circulating in the oceans. Immediately after a coastal disaster that may be true. But the ocean quickly breaks big stuff down and disburses it. There are high concentrations in ocean centers due to winds and the Coriolis force. The Coriolis force, whose existence is based on the rotation of spherical earth, pushes stuff to the right of the wind in the northern hemisphere. In the southern hemisphere winds blow stuff to the left. Winds in the temperate climates come from the west, so these winds push surface trash to the center. Trade winds, going in the other direction, also push the trash towards the center. And so it accumulates.

Several commercial and nonprofit groups are developing techniques for cleaning up the ocean. The difficulties are operating in a very hostile environment, covering a huge area, and not using expensive fuels. Watch for developments in ocean clean up in the next few years.

Other things that are fun to see

Have you noticed parallel lines on the surface? Some of the lines you see are traces of ships or boats passing by. Near the mouth of a bay or harbor

you can sometimes see a "tideline." Seaweed and other floating material accumulates between two bodies of water, bay water and ocean water. Where river water enters the sea, the denser sea water slides beneath leaving any floating material in a line where the two waters meet. Other water movement such as convergence of water caused by eddies and internal waves can cause tidelines.

Where the waters of two rivers meet or where river water enters the sea you can often see clear distinction between them. This is the Rio Negro coming into the Amazon at Manaus, Brazil. Photo by Bill Yeaton.

Waves occur on the interface between fluids of different densities. The waves we commonly think of occur between the sea and air. But waves also occur between layers of seawater that have different densities. Polar explorer and Nobel Laurette, Fridtijof Nansen discovered them in on his famous Fram Expedition in 1893. His account, Farthest North, of this expedition in the Arctic Sea is a great read.

Windrows

When you see several lines that are parallel you are seeing "windrows." They occur when the wind speed

Parallel lines on the ocean are generated by light winds. As wind speed increases the lines will be lost in the confusion of the sea. Photo by Barbara Sobey.

Irving Langmuir, who figured out the cause for the parallel lines, was not an oceanographer or hydrodynamist, but a chemist. He was a clever chemist who won the 1932 Nobel Prize for his discoveries in surface chemistry.

is greater than 3 knots but less than twice that speed. At higher winds, waves destroy the lines. The parallel lines are the surface manifestations of Langmuir circulation. The wind sets up counter-rotating current vortices in the water that are nearly parallel to the wind. In the northern hemisphere the circulation and lines are a few degrees to the right of the wind.

The counter-rotating circulation, like two gears meshing, circulate water upward together. They move the surface water a few meters up to 300 meters away from each other, and then sink where they run into the next pair of vortices. Any oils, seaweed, or junk that has accompanied the sideways movement of the surface water accumulates above the downward sinking water between vortices. Standing on a ship you see the lines of accumulated materials stretching off as far as your eye can see.

How blue it is

Hold up a glass of ocean water and you'll see right through it. Aside from some bits of sand or maybe a tiny critter, the water is transparent.

But look over the side of a ship through a 200 or 2,000 m column of the same water and you see it's not transparent. You can't see far and instead of having no color the column is blue. What changed?

Water absorbs light. If you take an underwater camera below 30' the pictures will show you how low the ambient light levels are. And, the photos will show that much of the color, especially the reds and yellows, has disappeared. Water absorbs red wavelengths of light over a short distance.

The color that travels farthest in the water is blue. That blue light bounces off any particles in the water scattering blue light back to your eye. The color of the ocean appears blue.

In the shallow water of a tropical island sunlight retains all of its wavelengths before reflecting off the sandy bottom. The water doesn't appear blue; it's clear and you can see the white sand.

In the North Atlantic and other places that are rich in marine life and nutrients, the red and green wavelengths of light reflect off marine plants and animals near the surface, before they are absorbed by seawater. The reflected light will be blue-green. Where there is little life in the water, near coral reefs for instance, sunlight penetrates far absorbing the non-blue colors, leaving only blue light to scatter back.

So the ocean isn't always blue, but when it is blue it's due to the absorption of all the other colors of sunlight. The color absorbed last is blue light. Before it is absorbed, it reflects back to us so we see blue.

Clouds, too, affect ocean surface color. When sunlight reflects off a cloud at sunrise or sunset, the ocean takes on the richer colors of the cloud. Later in the day with the sun higher overhead, cloud shadows create dark patches on the ocean.

Ocean color also changes where rivers entering the sea bring with

So is the sky blue for the same reason? No. As solar light passes through the atmosphere blue wavelengths have the right length to scatter off molecules of oxygen and nitrogen, the principle gasses of the atmosphere. The blue light is reflected or scattered so we see blue.

At sunset solar light passes through a longer path in the atmosphere. The light has more opportunity to scatter off particles, letting more of the remaining red and orange wavelengths color the sky. We see more colorful sunsets.

Air pollution and volcano eruptions add sulfur aerosols that increase the scattering of reds and oranges. These polluted skies can generate even more vibrant sunsets.

them the eroded sediments from land. If the river water doesn't mixed with ocean water a green or brown plume can extend far into the ocean. The outflow from the Amazon River can be seen for over a hundred miles. Do a search for NASA satellite photos showing its extent.

Look up!

One of the cool things about being at sea is being able to see all the way to the horizon. No buildings, mountains, or trees to interrupt your view. This gives you a great view of the weather that you don't often get living on land, especially in a city.

Fall streaks or virga

Some days you can look around the ship to see several squalls or rain showers. As the ship approaches one

A squall at sea. If the rain doesn't reach the sea surface, it is called a fall streak or virga. Photo by Bill Yeaton.

you can see the sea surface change as it is pelted by rain.

You'll notice that in some squalls the rain never hits the ocean surface. It evaporates on its way down. This is called virga or fall streaks. You can see the straight dark lines of rainfall, but they evaporate before hitting the ocean.

Most rain, except in the tropics, starts as ice crystals. On its way down it melts into rain drops. As the drops fall they encounter higher atmospheric pressure and higher temperatures so the raindrops often evaporate. It's raining, but the rain doesn't get to the surface. On land you rarely notice this, but at sea you can.

Rainbows

Of course rain at sea brings great rainbows. With nothing blocking your line of sight, you can see full rainbows. And, there is an added bonus. The salt water blown off waves in a strong wind can cause a rainbow as well as a rain squall.

To view rainbows, your back will be toward the sun. The sun's rays hit raindrops, bend or refract entering the drop and reflect off the inside surfaces once or twice before coming back to you. When a ray of light reflects once inside a raindrop, the result is a single rainbow with the progression of color remembered as "ROYGBIV." That is red, orange, yellow, green, blue, indigo, and violet from the outer to the inner colors. The color positions are reversed in a double rainbow. The second rainbow of a double rainbow results from the second reflection inside the raindrop.

Watching clouds

The time you spend at sea is perfect for watching the clouds. You will have great views all around you, uninterrupted by buildings or mountains.

Watch the edges of the white, fluffy cumulus clouds. They constantly change, growing here and shrinking there. The water vapor that makes the clouds visible is evaporating and disappearing or condensing and appearing.

The perfect weather clouds you hope to see are the end result of the upward movement of water-laded air. The sun heats the water surface increasing the evaporation of water and warming the surface. The surface in turn heats the air it comes in contact with. This air, now warm and having high humidity from the evaporated water, rises. As it rises a few thousand feet it cools. When cooled, the water vapor condenses forming visible clouds.

All that air rising means there has to be air moving from the cloud level back to the sea surface. This downward moving air occurs in the clear skies between the cumulus clouds.

If the air rising off the ocean surface doesn't stop at the low cloud level, it builds towering clouds that rise up to the height of commercial aircraft. That huge vertical motion of moisture and heat is what breeds thunderstorms and other violent weather.

Also notice that higher clouds are moving in different direction than the low clouds do. The highest clouds are composed of ice crystals. These clouds don't block sunlight and don't provide moisture for rain, but they can foretell changing weather.

Between the highest and lowest clouds are sheet clouds (stratus) and cumulus (lumpy clouds). These are responsible for precipitation. See our section on forecasting below.

Fog

On land fog can form when the land surface cools overnight by radiating heat into the atmosphere. The land cools the air above it and water vapor condenses into fog. At sea, the surface doesn't cool much by radiation, but fog still forms when

Sea smoke formed in this Norwegian fjord as cool air descended from the mountains and moved over the warmer water.

moist air is cooled by moving over colder water. This is sea fog.

Different looking is sea smoke. Rather than a blanket of clouds on the surface it is wispy swirls of cloudy air floating above the water. It forms when very cold air passes over warmer waters.

Lightning

Yes, lightning does occur at sea. Generally there are fewer lightning strikes at sea than ashore. Regions of high lightning activity include the Gulf of Mexico and along the east coast of the U.S., the equatorial west coast of Africa, and the southern coast of Brazil and Argentina. Throughout much of the ocean the occurrence of strikes is 1/5 as frequent or less.

Lightning does hit boats and ships. Vessels need to be grounded to be safe. As a passenger you are reasonably safe, but you do not want to stand on the deck when lightning is about. To judge the distance to a strike, count the seconds between the

Lightning does occur at sea. However your ship is grounded by its contact with ocean water. In a small boat a lightning strike can be severely dangerous. Some sailors recommend putting small essential electronic devices inside a microwave oven to keep them safe. Everyone should be off the deck if possible. Fishing rods should be stowed. Photo by Will Hayes.

On warm sultry days watch for waterspouts. They usually don't do much damage, but you don't want to be near them. Take a photo from far away. Photo by Will Hayes.

flash and the sound. Since light travels so fast you see the strike essentially the instant it occurs. Sound, however, pokes along at 5 seconds per mile. So for every five seconds of time elapsed between seeing and hearing the lightning strike is one mile distance between you and the lightning.

Waterspouts

When the best word that describes the air outside is sultry, be on the lookout for waterspouts. More common in tropical or subtropical waters, they can form anywhere. Most are associated with fair weather clouds, but the more dangerous type are associated with strong weather systems.

On said sultry day watch as the cumulus clouds grow taller and the sky darkens. The underside of the clouds is ragged indicating unstable air movements. Moist air is rising higher and higher. At the edge of clouds look for the start of a funnel shape. If it matures and grows downward you will see a bright patch on the surface of water beneath it.

The funnel grows downward. What you see is condensation formed by the lower pressure inside the rapidly spinning funnel. If the funnel touches the surface you will see spray flung upwards.

The fair weather waterspouts often don't move much and don't cause much damage. Usually. They are not likely to chase you all over the ocean. If they do run inside your ship, the deck furniture will be blown about. Not to make too much light of such an encounter, you do want to get indoors to avoid flying debris. In a small boat avoid them.

Waterspouts don't last long. If you have to run below to get your camera it will likely be gone by the time you return. Of course atmospheric conditions won't change in a few minutes and another spout could start.

Sunsets and the Green Flash

How many sunset photos will you take on your cruise? Probably one more than your neighbors want to see. But watching the sun dip below the unobstructed horizon and capturing it in photos is one of the allures of spending time at sea.

With the sun high in the sky, solar light travels a short distance through earth's atmosphere. The oxygen and nitrogen molecules in the atmosphere scatter smaller wavelengths of light painting the sky blue.

At sunset solar light travels through a much longer section of atmosphere. The blue short wavelength light is scattered and removed long before sunlight reaches your eyeballs. The light remaining is from the longer wavelengths, yellows and reds. The sunset will be nice, but not spectacular.

Just one more sunset photo. Photo by Bill Yeaton.

Add particles from a forest fire, volcanic eruption, or even sea spray and the sunset can be truly picturesque. Other sources of particles unfortunately are human-generated. Air pollution from cars and factory smokestacks can colorize sunsets.

And, the Green Flash? Yes, it does occur, but not as often as you'd like. You need a clear view of the horizon as the sun is setting, with no clouds and a stable atmosphere. Sunlight is bent or refracted as it passes through the atmosphere. Short wavelengths, blue and green, bend more than longer wavelength reds and yellows.

As the sun sets sunlight has to pass through more of the earth's atmosphere before it reaches you. Blue wavelengths are scattered from the light leaving more red, orange, and yellow wavelengths. Photo by Bill Yeaton.

So as the sun sets below the horizon you continue to see its image because the light is bent. The longer wavelength light, reds and oranges, don't bend as much and fall short of your position. So the light reaching you from the sun now below the horizon doesn't have red and yellow light. The colors with the most bend, green and blue, are the last to disappear. But blue light scatters much more than green, leaving only green. So the final gasp of the sunset is a green flash of light.

It lasts a fraction of a second. But if you see it, race like crazy to the next highest deck to see if you can view it again. Scoring a double green flash would be a Facebook moment for sure.

Celestial views

You can see far beyond the atmosphere and a cruise at sea offers opportunities for un-paralleled viewing of the sky. Do you notice the moon during the day when you are at home? Check it out at sea. Watch the different shape and position each day. It will rise about 50 minutes later each day. Tides, which are largely controlled by the gravitational pull of the moon, are 50 minutes later each day too.

Full moon and new moon generate the largest tides, called spring tides. These conditions occur when the sun, earth, and moon are all aligned in a straight line. The gravitational attraction of the sun and moon reinforce each other. The opposite conditions is called neap tides. The moon rises or sets when the sun is highest in the sky or in the middle of the night.

The International Space Station (ISS) can be seen during the day or night. It moves quickly across the sky and is quite bright. NASA has an interactive map and an email alert to help spot the ISS called "spot the station."

Planets can be seen during the day as well as night. Check out apps that will give current locations.

The rays of sunlight filtering through the clouds are called Crepuscular rays. Photo by Bill Yeaton.

At night go on deck to see great views of stars. You might ask the cruise director to have the ship's non-navigational lights turned off for half an hour so passengers can enjoy the sky. For people from the Northern Hemisphere seeing the Southern Cross is a treat. You don't have to be in the Southern Hemisphere to see it. It can be seen as far north as 25 degrees North Latitude. Locations near Hawaii and the Caribbean can see it. At this latitude it is quite low and difficult to see above the horizon. Spring is the best time to see it from the Northern Hemisphere. The Southern Cross, or Crux, is not directly south, but is close to south.

Ice on the ocean

You are someplace very special if you get to see ice on the ocean. There are two types of ocean ice: icebergs and sea ice.

Icebergs

The ship will not get close to icebergs, but you can still be close enough for a good view. Icebergs are hunks of glaciers that have been pushed into the sea. They form from snow being compacted into ice over many years. Glaciers slide down to the sea from higher elevations, dragging rocks with them.

Sailing into a fjord you can see the piles of rocks they have left behind along their sides (lateral moraines) and at the end (terminal moraine).

A bergy bit from one of the glaciers in Prince William Sound. Photo by Barbara Sobey

Where the terminal moraine is underwater, it forms a sill that limits water circulation in the fjord.

Since icebergs form from precipitation their ice is fresh. Being less dense than the surrounding salty sea, icebergs float. But they only expose about 10% of their mass.

The best place to see icebergs is Greenland and in Iceberg Alley, between Greenland and Newfoundland. It was an iceberg from this region that sank the Titanic.

Other places to see icebergs are Prince William Sound and Glacier

An iceberg near the Antarctic peninsula. Photo by Charles Ford.

Bay, Alaska; and Patagonia, South America. If you cruise to the Antarctic Peninsula or Antarctic islands you undoubtedly will see icebergs.

A small iceberg south of Greenland. Photo by Barbara Sobey.

Look closely at icebergs with binoculars. You might see birds resting or even seals hauling out on the ice. Look at the water color around the berg. Does it look different than the surrounding water? Nutrients released from bergs allow plankton blooms to form.

To be called an iceberg a piece of fresh water ice must project at least 16' above the sea surface and must be greater than 5,000 square feet, roughly 1/8 of an acre. Smaller bits are called bergy bits, projecting 3 – 16' above the sea surface, and growlers, about the size of a truck.

Icebergs that form from ice sheets are flat topped. Those that form from glaciers are irregular in shape. Most of the bergs in the Arctic form from glaciers on Greenland and are irregular. Most of the bergs in the Antarctic form from giant ice sheets that get pushed into the ocean and have flat tops. These can be huge: as large as a small U.S. state. Where would we be without Rhode Island to compare to icebergs?

Sea ice

Yes, salt water does freeze. The water has to be cooled to 28 degrees F or -2 degrees C before it freezes. Freezing seawater forms small plates that join to give a glassy appearance to the surface if there is no wind. With wind the plates smash together to give the surface a greasy appearance. If the air temperature is cold enough pancakes form and these eventually freeze into large sheets. Ice continues to grow outward and downward. It takes a full winter season for the ice to grow 5 or 6' thick. If the ice survives over the following summer, it continues to thicken.

Ocean water freezes when cooled to about -2 degrees centigrade. As ice crystals form they eject salt so sea ice slowly becomes fresher. This spring time photo shows sea ice breaking up in the Bering Sea and algae starting to grow. Photo by Carol Ladd.

This isn't the smooth ice of an ice skating rink. Wind and tides break the ice into chunks that collide with each other and rub against each other.

Look for holes in the ice. In the far south, round holes are breathing holes for seals. Long cracks show where ice sheets have broken apart.

In the Arctic global warming is fast shrinking the area covered by sea ice. The Arctic will be ice free in a few years. Then it is unlikely to return to a sea ice covered ocean for many years. Around Antarctica sea ice is thinning. Soon, I predict, the area covered by sea ice each winter will start to shrink dramatically.

In the Arctic sea ice can be several years old. This ice can be scrunched into ridges several meters tall. The accounts of Arctic explorers tell tales of excruciating travails in navigating through and across the sea ice. It could take all day to go just a few miles. Antarctic sea ice, not confined by surrounding continents as is in the Arctic, breaks apart every spring and melts leaving almost no multi-year ice.

Chapter 8

Land Ho!

AFTER A FEW DAYS AT SEA MOST PEOPLE ARE anxious to see land. As the ship draws closer look at the features of the land. Take note of the shape of islands or other lands. The shape suggests how that piece of land formed or what the dominant geologic features are.

Often you will see a band of clouds on the horizon before land appears. Moist sea air rises as it is pushed ashore. The rising air condenses to form clouds. Distant clouds on an otherwise cloudless day are no guarantee of land, but they are a hint that land may be there.

Volcanoes surround the Pacific Ocean giving rise to the name "ring of fire." As the giant Pacific tectonic plate is pushed under the surrounding tectonic plates, volcanoes form. Sailing into the west coast ports along Oregon, Washington, British Columbia, and Alaska, you see the volcanic mountains. Throughout most of the year they are snow or glacier covered. Similar land forms occur in Japan. Sailing into Tokyo Bay on a clear day gives beautiful views of Mt. Fuji even though it is 80 miles away.

Volcanic Mt. Fuji rises above the land and presents a perfect welcome into Tokyo Bay. Photo by Barbara Sobey.

Islands

Few things are as beautiful as an island rising out of the middle of the ocean. Why is that island there? Islands pop up for one of three reasons. A few are really pieces of the nearest mainland that got separated during recent sea level rise. Sea level rose after the last glacial maximum about 20,000 years ago. The glaciers melted and the melt water flowed into the ocean. Today sea level stands about 425' higher than it did during the glacial period.

So some islands today used to be attached to continents in the glacial age. Rising sea level inundated the area between them. Trinidad in the Caribbean is an example. It is geologically a piece of Venezuela, now separated by 7 miles of ocean.

Volcanoes are responsible for many oceanic islands. The Hawaiian Islands and French Polynesia are two examples. Many of the Caribbean islands were or are volcanoes. St. Lucia, with its Piton Mountains, shows its volcanic origin.

This pair of volcanic spires rises 2,500' above the Caribbean Sea on St. Lucia.

Cruising in the Caribbean you encounter both volcanic and non-volcanic islands. St. Lucia has its Pitons, but Barbados doesn't have a volcano. Barbados represents a third type of island. From a map of the Caribbean you can see that Barbados is located outside the semi-circular

Sea level continues to rise and at a very fast pace today. This is a good time to sell that water-front property. As earth's temperature rises, glaciers around the world melt. What matters most are the glaciers on Antarctica and Greenland, as they hold vast quantities of frozen water. While the glaciers are shrinking, the oceans are warming. Seawater expands as it warms. The double whammy of more water and warmer water is already causing problems for east coast cities like Miami and Boston.

ring of volcanic islands of the Lesser Antilles. As you sail into Barbados you'll not see a volcanic peak.

Barbados sits atop the junction of two tectonic plates, the Caribbean and South American. As the South American plate is forced downward under the Caribbean plate, it bulldozes sediment up to make the island. Barbados is an island made from one tectonic plate scraping sediment off the top of another.

Volcanic islands and atolls

Volcanic mountain islands are scattered throughout the world ocean, especially in the Pacific. The solid rock rises straight out of the ocean and summits in one or more volcanic peaks. The big island of Hawaii has five ancient and active volcanoes.

If your cruise continues along an island chain like French Polynesia or Hawaii you will be traveling back in time. The farther you travel westward from the active volcano in the chain, the older the islands are. Check out a chart of the ocean to see the trail of islands starting in Hawaii. This chain stretches westward across the Pacific Ocean for thousands of miles. Let your finger follow the islands and seamounts (now submerged volcanoes) across the Pacific. As your finger moves across the ocean each island it encounters is older.

Steam clouds arise out of the volcano Stromboli. This is one of three active volcanoes in Italy. The volcano and the island it forms are in the Tyrrhenian Sea, part of the Mediterranean Sea. Photo by Bill Yeaton.

The islands and seamounts form a straight line until you hit the Emperor Seamounts. Just west of the International Date Line the chain turns northward. This bend represents a change of direction of the Pacific tectonic plate that occurred about 50 million years ago.

Because the Pacific plate moves westward, the youngest island in these chains is at the eastern end. Each adjacent island to the west is a few million years older and more eroded.

Sailing west from Tahiti, which is at the eastern end of a French Polynesia chain of islands, you can see he progression.

High volcanic islands force air currents to rise and rain to fall. These "high islands" support diverse life. On "low islands" rain and water are hard to come by. You'll notice ashore that houses collect any rain water from their roofs and store it in cisterns.

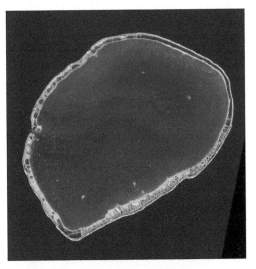

The volcano that formed the original island has now sunk beneath the sea surface leaving the surrounding ring of coral reefs and motus or islands. This is Tikehau Atoll in French Polynesia. Photo by NASA.

Creating these islands is lava from the earth's mantle. In some spots, "hotspots," lava rises for millions of years. It can turn on and off creating islands that move away as the tectonic plate slides. Image a factory turning out a part that drops onto a conveyor belt. The island of Hawaii is where the part is produced. Its conveyor belt stretches across the

Pacific, moving a few centimeters a year.

Traveling along an island chain you can see the results of geologic forces. For example, the magma hot spot east of Tahiti is where the future condos will arise – in a million years or so. Tahiti itself is a high island (7,352') with dramatic landscapes and a fringing reef. There is no lagoon.

A few miles away is beautiful Moorea. This island is a bit older and not as tall (3,960'). Farther still is Bora Bora. It's shorter (2,385') and has a huge lagoon. The island has been eroded and has sunk. As it sunk the surrounding coral reef grew. It kept pace with the sinking land so now forms a barrier reef around the island. Bora Bora is not yet an atoll, but it will become one.

Bora Bora, one of the most beautiful islands in the world, is a near atoll. Photo by Bill Yeaton.

Atolls form from volcanic islands, but you don't see the volcano. It has shrunk below the ocean surface. The weight of the island depresses the sea floor and erosion reduces the height of the volcano. Eventually the volcano top disappears. What

was once a coral reef surrounding the volcano is now a barrier reef, all that remains of the island.

If your ship enters the lagoon of an atoll be sure to be on deck. Watch the pattern of waves indicate the channel the ship should use. As waves crash on the reef they throw up lines of white water. But at the channel mouth the waves don't break. The water is deeper there so the waves don't build and break. Unless the opening is dredged it will remain open only as long it provides an escape for fresh water from the lagoon. The freshwater outflow kills the reef-building corals. Over time the island sinks so it gets less orographic rainfall. When the supply of rainfall diminishes, the corals will close off the channel.

If the volcano sinks faster than coral can grow, it will disappear entirely. As it sinks, waves wash over the summit and erode the mountain into a flat top. There are fewer than 300 of these "guyots" or flat-topped seamounts in the world. Most are in the Pacific Ocean.

Not all volcanoes become islands. Many rise up from the ocean floor, grow, and then stop before reaching the sea surface. These submarine volcanoes are called "seamounts." There are nearly 10,000 of them scattered throughout the world ocean, but again most are in the North Pacific. A close look at a nautical chart will reveal these features, many of which have been named. You would think that we would know the locations of these features exactly, but not so. The USS San Francisco, a submarine, ran into a submerged mountain in 2005. The mountain was not shown on their navigational chart.

White cliffs

Cruising the North Atlantic Ocean past the White Cliffs of Dover, or better still the Seven Sisters, you are confronted by a wall of sedimentary rock hundreds of feet high. No volcanoes here. The cliffs represent millions of years of deposits of an algae that grows a shell of calcium carbonate.

The shells pile up at about the same rate dust settles on your bookcase at home. Later geological forces raised the accumulated sediments and later still the face was trimmed by giant floods. Today these cliffs erode about 1 cm per year.

These white cliffs of the Seven Sisters are composed of billions of shells of microscopic marine plants that were later uplifted and then shaped by floods. These cliffs are near the better known White Cliffs of Dover. Photo by Barbara Sobey.

Fjords

Norway, New Zealand, Iceland, Greenland, Southeast Alaska, and Chile are home to fjords. Glaciers eroded the mountains forming fjords. Glacial melt water flows into the fjords making a nearly freshwater layer on top of seawater. Sailing into a fjord is a special treat. The open expanse of the sea has been replaced by the tightly confined walls. At times you could almost reach out to touch a passing wall.

A glacier meets the sea in this fjord in Chile.

Looking up the valley sides you can see where glaciers once eroded their valley. The valleys are shaped as the letter "U." In contrast river valleys have a "V" shape. You may see piles of rocks pushed by the glaciers. These moraines can be found at the terminal end of the glacier, a terminal moraine, and along the sides of a glacier, lateral moraines.

Cruise ship stops are made usually only at the head of the fjord. That is the only place where there is access to the land. The fjord walls are nearly vertical and offer few bays for landing. The towns are situated at the fjord head along streams or rivers that follow the path of the glacier.

Small rocky islands or reefs mark the entrance to many fjords. These are glacially cut features. Photo by Barbara Sobey.

In the sea just outside of fjords you often see low rocky islands aligned with the direction of the fjord. The name for such islands is skerry. They were created by glaciers moving down fjords and rising sea level. You can see them along the Inside Passage to Alaska and along the coasts of Norwegian, Iceland, Sweden, Finland, and the United Kingdom.

Glaciers cut distinctive "U" valleys. This one is in Norway.

Waves and the coast

Watch waves as they move from the open ocean toward the shore. They may come from storms thousands of miles away from any open direction. As they encounter shallow water the waves slow down. The ones behind almost catch up to the ones in front. With more wave energy in a shorter wavelength, the crests rise. Eventually the crest will be so high that it topples over. This occurs when the height of the wave is 1/7 of the wave length (distance from one wave crest to the next).

Gently sloping beaches with sand suggest that wave energy is low and that there is a supply of sand nearby. This is Maracas Beach in Brazil. Photo by Bill Yeaton.

As the long line of waves comes to shore it bends. Although the storm that generated the waves might lie far to the north or south, as the waves near the shore they bend so they are nearly parallel to the shore. When they finally hit the shore, they may appear to be parallel.

But nearly parallel isn't parallel. The waves won't break at the same instant along a beach. They will break at one end of the beach first and then break farther down the beach.

Waves coming into a beach at this slight angle causes a current along the shore. As the waves crash and the turbulence picks up sand, the current moves that sand alongshore. This movement of sediment along the shore erodes some areas and deposits sand in others. Sand spits at the mouth of a bay or harbor are generated by this movement of sand.

High wave energy cuts away at the rocky headlands in the Shetland Islands. Beaches are carried away by the waves and currents.

Beach front property owners want to protect their beaches from erosion. So they build protective structures into the surf zone to block the alongshore flow. These piles of rocks or pilings are called groins. Along some beaches you can see a series of groins. As one person tries to block the alongshore flow of sand, it piles up on the upstream side of his groin. But robbed of the sand, his neighbor on the downstream side watches his beach wash away. So this neighbor also builds a groin. This continues down the beach transforming a natural looking beach into a strange scalloped-shaped beach with groins sticking out into the ocean.

Long spits of land, as occur along the eastern U.S., tell us that the sand is being carried by currents. This process continues today and suggests that these beach front properties are ephemeral. Your second happiest day will be when you purchase such property; your happiest day will be when someone else inherits the inevitable disaster of a winter storm washing it all away.

Rocky coast lines tell you that the coast is exposed to high wave energy. The waves have stirred up and removed any sand. Sheer rock cliffs occur where tectonic forces are lifting the land. On the big island of Hawaii you may see the rocky coastline created as lava from Kilauea volcano flows into the sea.

Waves erode rocky headlands creating beautiful sea stacks, sea arches, and caves. The erosion-resistant rock remains after more easily eroded material has been washed away. More wave energy focuses on the rocky ridges projecting into the ocean. Eventually the waves with break through leaving spires of rock (sea stacks) or holes through the ridge (sea arches).

Chapter 9

Things to See Onboard

A visit to the bridge

SECURITY CONCERNS HAVE MADE BRIDGE TOURS more restrictive in recent years. If a ship offers them at all you need to sign up well in advance of the tour. You meet in a group and are led to the bridge where the officer of the watch will show you around. It can be a great experience.

One of the first things you notice on the bridge is that, except for your group of passengers, the bridge is almost deserted. There may be only one officer and one crew.

You also notice there is no steering wheel. Looking closer you can find a

Some ships will allow passengers onto the bridge any time. Most, however, organize bridge tours. Photo by Barbara Sobey.

tiny steering wheel that is not used at sea.

Steering wheels for ships and boats are relatively new technology. Early ships, like Viking ships, were steered with a steering oar. Ancient Chinese, Romans, and Arab sailors used rudders on some ships, but it wasn't until the 14th century that the modern rudder as invented. In Europe and the Middle East a hinged rudder was mounted on a vertical stern post and controlled by ropes on either side.

Wood handles attached to the rudder, called tillers, allowed for direct control by the steersman. But as ships got larger it became more difficult for the steersman to be close to the rudder and be able to see the sails. Since most navigating at sea was by setting the sails for the intended course and then steering to keep the sails full, the steersman had to see the sails.

Instead of the large ship's wheel with a sailor guiding its movements, modern ships are tiny wheels that are rarely used at sea. Ryan Bent Photography.

The ship's wheel was invented in the early 18th century. As any new technology it took a few years to catch on, but by mid-century ships had wheels. Three centuries later, they are a relic for large ships.

Steering at sea is a task for computers. No sailor is involved. The course is entered into the navigation computer, which also keeps track of progress using GPS. Computer displays show the real-time position of the ship and how close it is to its programmed track.

Look at the navigation display. If there any ships within miles they will show up on the display. In the old days, the mate on watch would radio call to another ship if there was any confusion about how the ships would pass each other. Of course the mate couldn't read the name of the ship so when he called on radio channel 16 he had to say something like: "This is the motor vessel Enterprise calling a tanker near" such and such a location. Once contact was established protocol calls for the mates on the two ships to switch to a less-used channel to talk about who was going where.

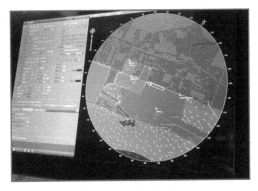

The navigation system displays the position of your ship and all ships nearby. By clicking on one of the ships information is given on its name, home port, ship type, speed and direction, and destination.

Looking on the navigation screen you see not only the position of every ship within your vicinity, you also see the names of the ships, their course and speed. By clicking the mouse on the ship's symbol all the other information on that ship comes up: their destination, their last port, etc. At sea this is quite handy. In a crowded port with dozens of ships maneuvering it is a godsend.

You can get much of this information from an on-line service called Marine Traffic. Friends and family back home can follow your ship on this service. You can identify interesting ships in port or close to shore. Far out to sea the free service isn't available.

The ship operates radar all the time the ship is at sea. It probably has three different radar units working all the time. Above the bridge you can see three spinning antennas, each of a different size. Each one provides radar images of a different wavelength for different distances. One display in the bridge shows the radar images. The mate can switch that display from the close to the far range.

One machine will show the latest weather forecast. Cruise ship companies engage weather forecasting services to send them weather reports and forecasts.

A great weather service for you to use is **Passage Weather**. You select the area of the ocean and it will show you wind, wave, atmospheric pressure, visibility, and precipitation forecasts.

Other displays show how many diesel engines are on-line. Some ships are propelled by diesel engines and some are propelled by electric motors, powered by diesel engines. The engines also provide enough electricity to make fresh water, heat, and air conditioning, and provide power for a thousand other uses. The mate on watch can pull up a display to show power consumption, fresh water production, and fire and other alarms throughout the ship.

Two or three of the bridge windows will have circular windshield wipers. These wipers operate at very high speed and do a good job of providing visibility when rain and sea spray would otherwise blind the watch.

With no second-by-second work to do, it would be easy for the bridge watch to wander away or take a nap. Except that every few minutes an alarm sounds that someone must physically stop before it alerts the captain.

You might also notice no nautical charts. The ship might have them, but navigation is done now using computers. The officers still learn how to use charts and sextants, but rarely use either.

Look for an inclinometer. It measures the port to starboard tilt of the ship. It is a pendulum mounted athwart ships. You might ask the mate what was the biggest roll he has ever seen.

Inclinometers show the angle of list or lean to one side. This one uses a bubble in a fluid filled glass tube. Another style is a pendulum. Inclinometers are mounted athwart ships and high on a bulkhead.

Somewhere will be a pigeonhole cabinet containing the signal flags. Aside from the pilot aboard flag and the quarantine flag (solid yellow), these aren't used often. There is a dictionary of phrases that ships used to use and still could that employ combinations of flags. Urgent messages require one flag, less urgent messages use a combination of two or more flags. You can send any short message using the flags, but it is fast becoming a lost art.

One panel inside the bridge has controls for bow and stern thrusters. Each thruster is controlled by a single lever. The controls are duplicated on each wing so the captain can operate

the thruster while standing close to the dock.

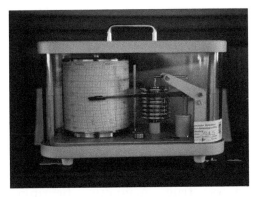

A recording barometer or barograph is one of the instruments seen on a bridge. Ryan Bent Photography.

Navigational compasses are on the bridge and wings. They are mounted in a vertical post called a binnacle. The old style binnacle

A relic from the past, signal flags are not used in many situations today. Flags are used to indicate that a pilot is aboard, that fuel is being loaded, that a pratique or health inspection is requested, and when divers are working underwater.

On top of a compass on the bridge you may see a sighting device called a pelorius. A mate can sight through to align it with an object of interest and read the compass direction.

On some bridge tours the helpful person who took you to bridge will be anxious to get you off the bridge. Other times the watch officer may enjoy having company and as long as you are asking questions you might be allowed to stay.

Most modern ships have bow and stern thrusters to make maneuvering easier. The cost of building these electric motors into the ship is partly offset by not having to hire tugboats.

has a pair of iron balls, called the navigator's balls, mounted on either side of the compass. These balls can be moved closer or farther away from the compass to compensate for magnetic fields from the ship and its equipment so the compass shows true magnetic bearings. The magnetic compasses must be certified periodically. A technician comes aboard and checks the compass while the ship is rotated to each of cardinal compass points. The technician compares the compass to the GPS heading and adjusts metal tabs inside the binnacle to make them align.

There is also a depth sounder operating full time. The saying is often made that we know the surface of the moon better than the surface of our own ocean. There aren't many big surprises hiding under the sea, but there are lots of smaller ones and the sonar is a last line of defense.

As a general rule during the tour don't touch anything or sit down. Be a courteous guest and maybe you will be invited back.

Periodic adjustments need to be made to magnetic compasses to keep them aligned properly. A technician is adjusting metal tabs in the binnacle while the ship points in different directions.

Engine room tour

It is a rare opportunity to tour the engine room. If traveling on a cargo ship or private yacht you are more likely to be invited. Most likely what you will see is an immaculate space with noisy machinery providing electrical power, propulsion, water, and hot and cold air.

The huge spinning shaft connects a diesel engine to the ships propeller. Photo by Will Hayes.

There is a great variety in the types of propulsion used in ships and boats. Most common are diesel engines either directly driving propellers or driving electrical generators that provide power to electric motors. Most ships have several diesel engines, but usually only one or two are used at any one time. To travel at top speed requires the power of more of these engines and that drives up fuel expenses. Another diesel engine will drive the generator that provides electric power for all the ship's needs.

Be aware of that the electricity you use at home may be different from the power provided at sea. The voltage can be different (220v instead of 110v) and the frequency is often different (50 Hz instead of 60 Hz). The latter is important only if you're plugging in an electric clock.

During an engine room tour you might ask how fresh water is made. Some ships will load fresh water in port. But most have to make fresh water from salt water. They can boil the salt water, using heat from the engines and heat from a boiler. Or, they can use reverse osmosis to push the water through micro filters to remove the salt.

Not everyone would want to do a tour of the engine room, but for maritime geeks this is heaven. If your vision of an engine room is covered with grease, oil, and tools scattered about you will be in for a big surprise. Will Hayes.

Ask, too, about the treatment of waste and waste water. Laws govern where the ship can discharge gray water (from showers and sinks) and black water (from toilets). Ships do get caught making discharges in the wrong places and they pay a hefty fine.

Engine rooms contain an amazing complexity and diversity of technology. The mates who manage it have strong technical backgrounds that may quickly make your head spin. A tour is a treat that should not be missed.

And if an engine room tour is important, try booking a cruise on a cargo ship rather than a cruise ship. You will have a better chance for unlimited trips to the bridge and an occasional trip to the engine room.

Can you hear me now?

Ships carry a maze of electronic gear. On deck you can see the antennas that catch electronic signals for this gear.

Getting ready to get underway and at all times when at sea the radar antenna will be spinning. Most cruise ships have three radar antennas, one stacked above the next. The size of the antenna fits the wavelength of the radar (microwave) signal it transmits. So the three sizes represent three different wavelengths. Smaller wavelengths can see smaller objects, but they can't travel as far. If you get to go on a bridge tour, ask the mate

Most cruise ships operate three radar systems, each one designed for a different range. At sea you will see these spinning all the time. Most often they are mounted directly above the bridge.

to switch scales on the radar receiver so you can see the different ranges.

The radar sends out a microwave that bounces off ships and rocky headlands. Some of the reflected waves are detected by the spinning antenna. The radar electronics compute how far away the ship or headland is by measuring the time from when it sent out a signal to when it returned. If the target ship is big, more of the microwaves are reflected back and the image appears brighter on the radar screen.

If you're near a coastline when you visit the bridge, ask the mate to display the radar image of the coast line. You can see the bays and inlets. Before GPS, radar was used heavily for coastal navigation.

There are several "whip" antennas on the upper decks. These collect high frequency radio signals for communication. If a mate walks by when you are on the deck you might ask what each is for, but the odds are he doesn't know. There are electronic engineers who work for the Chief Engineer who maintain these antennas. The deck officers don't.

The other thing to notice are the large radar domes. These fiberglass structures are covers for a parabolic antennas inside. The covers protect the antenna and the motors that turn the antenna from the weather. These antennas pick up television, internet, and other signals coming from satellites. The ship is rolling, pitching, and yawing in and out of alignment with the satellite it's exchanging signals with. To keep the signals coming, the antenna moves to counteract the ship's motion. You will notice in really stormy weather

The large spherical domes protect the antenna inside from the elements. The antenna has to move to stay aligned with satellites to receive internet and television signals.

that television and internet signals are often lost. The antenna can't keep up with the ship's movements.

A smaller dome houses the GPS receiver. The Global Positioning System has revolutionized marine navigation. Printed paper charts are disappearing from pilot houses; charts are all digital. Noon sextant sightings of the sun and use of the compass are going away as well. Ask a mate when he last used a sextant.

GPS is based on knowing time and satellite positions to a high degree of accuracy. GPS satellites orbit the earth constantly broadcasting time signals. Receivers in ships (and cars, airplanes, and hand-held devices) receive the time broadcasts from four (of about two dozen) satellites. Knowing exactly where each satellite is and how long it took the signal to get from that satellite to the receiver, a GPS unit calculates its position.

Cruise ships show their position on the television channels available in your cabin. Some also show the ship's position on a digital map.

What's in the canisters?

As you stroll around the promenade deck you see several to many white fiberglass canisters secured to the deck. They are stowed outboard of the railings so people won't walk into them. These are your life rafts.

In case of sinking, these release automatically after coming in contact with water. You may be able to see the hydrostatic release. It is a small circular device attached to each life raft.

These white cylinders pop open when immersed in water. They supplement the life boats.

The good news is that you don't have to squeeze into the fiberglass canister in the event of a sinking. The release opens, the canister opens, and a tank of compressed air fills the life raft inside. These rafts are redundant safety features as in an emergency abandon ship the crew will endeavour to get everyone in a tender or life boat instead of a life raft.

Lifeboats

They are hung from davits on both sides of the ship. Although they would be crowded in an emergency, collectively they can handle all the passengers and crew. That's a big improvement since the sailing of the Titanic.

Lifeboats in most cases are tenders. Tenders are used to ferry passengers into ports that don't have adequate docking space. This happens when ports are crowded, where there is no dock, or where the bay isn't deep enough for the ship. The lifeboats are seaworthy and although they would be uncomfortable in storm waves they would save your life.

Life ring

Those bright orange rings mounted around the weather decks are rarely

This is a free-fall lifeboat used on commercial ships.

Each life raft has a release like this. When the release gets into the sea it allows the life raft to open and inflate.

used. But they could save a life. If someone falls or jumps overboard it can be difficult to find them, especially if the seas are not flat calm. Tossing in a life ring to mark the location not only provides some flotation for the person, it also makes them easier to see. Of course the bridge must be notified immediately. Have you memorized the phone number?

Rarely does a man-overboard happen. But it can. In the unlikely event you see one there are two things to do. Mark the spot by tossing in a life ring and notify the bridge. If there are two or more people have several stare intently at the person in the water while someone runs to tell the bridge.

Chapter 10

Special Places

Crossing the equator

I F YOU ARE A TRUSTY SHELLBACK YOU KNOW THE secret passage into Neptune's realm. But if you are lowly pollywog – if you don't know which you are, you're a pollywog – the mysteries will be revealed to you as you cross the equator on a ship.

The ceremony says a lot about the culture of the cruise line or ship you're riding. Some will play up the crossing and try to get everyone involved. For others it's just more work and they prefer to have you be spectators rather than participants.

All in good fun with no physical danger or embarrassment.

Someone will ask you when you get home from your equator-crossing cruise if you noticed the

King Neptune visits a cruise ship as it crosses the equator and invites lowly pollywogs to join the fraternity of shellbacks. Photo by Barbara Sobey.

My first equator crossing was while serving in the U.S. Navy aboard the USNS Michelson, a World War II victory ship. We were doing oceanographic surveys in the western pacific in the 1970s. There were just a handful of us pollywogs and I was the only officer pollywog. The crew took delight to getting their licks in on all of us pollywogs and especially me. The initiation was a bit rougher and certainly more humiliating than a cruise ship initiation. But I am a proud and trusty shellback.

direction water drained from your bathroom sink. To prepare yourself fill the basin and few days before the crossing, pull the plug, and watch the water drain. Note the direction of flow. Repeat this experiment a few days after the crossing. I suggest taking a few photos so you can show whoever asks.

Spoiler alert: water does not drain in the opposite direction when you cross the equator. The forces that cause storms and ocean gyres to swirl in opposite directions in the northern and southern hemispheres are too weak to influence the water draining in your sink. Check out a world map or map of the oceans to see the clockwise rotation of currents in the northern hemisphere and counterclockwise rotation in the southern hemisphere. On scales of hundreds to thousands of miles the earth's rotation (Coriolis force) influences the direction of water flow, but not over a scale of a few inches in your basin.

Crossing the Equator at the Prime Meridian

Crossing the equator aboard a ship is cool. Crossing at the zero or prime meridian is even cooler. The prime meridian is the line of longitude that passes through the Greenwich Observatory, east of London, and is the line of zero longitude.

The intersection of the Prime Meridian and the Equator is 00 00 in the Gulf of Guinea. Photo by Barbara Sobey.

The 00 00 point is in the Gulf of Guinea, off the west coast of Africa. Our Semester at Sea captain liked to pass through this point even though it took us out of the way. As we got close one of my students yelled out that he saw a buoy. And sure enough in thousands of feet of water there was a NOAA buoy collecting meteorological and oceanographic data. It is one of a large number of buoys NOAA maintains for research and weather predictions. So there is a marker at the 00 00 point.

Crossing the equator on a ship makes you a shellback. Crossing it at the Prime Meridian makes you an emerald shellback!

The International Date Line

Most ships don't make a big deal about crossing the date line. But it does confuse everyone. The first people to sail around the world, Magellan's crew (Magellan died along the way), didn't realize they had crossed a date line. When they finally got home their ship's log was one day off from the correct date. This inconsistency must have required a clever person to figure out. We're still confused.

To add to the confusion the date line is not a straight line. Although the prime meridian at 0 degrees of longitude is a nice, straight line, its counterpart nominally at 180 degrees on the other side of the world is a convoluted mess.

Each country that is bisected by the line chooses which side they are on. The Samoan Islands are located east of the 180 degree line so logically they would have the same date as Hawaii. But they have changed their date back and forth

by choosing which side of the date line they wanted to be on depending on who their major trading partners were. To make the switch they have to either drop a day from their calendar or add a day.

As you sail over the 180th meridian your ship's time may not change. The captain determines what the date and time are. He will probably set them to coincide with the time at the next port.

If you happen to cross the equator at the 180th meridian, not only do you become a trusty shellback. You become a Golden Shellback. This is a very rare honor that gives you serious bragging rights.

Arctic Circle

Crossing the Arctic Circle makes you eligible for yet another certificate. If you're on a small ship, maybe you can do an Arctic plunge. Most places you might cross are not marked, but along the Norwegian coast is a very

Crossing the Arctic Circle along the inside passage in Norway is marked by this monument.

Why not? Jump into the Arctic Ocean. Only a small percentage of the passengers and crew jump in, but most think it is a fun experience. Photo by Star Legend.

The most difficult task in building the Panama Canal was digging through the mountains to make the Culebra or Gaillard Cut. The Centennial Bridge is behind the cut. Ryan Bent Photography.

attractive statue to show the exact spot.

Panama Canal

Traversing the Panama Canal is another special treat. Although only about 50 miles in length, it takes all day to get through.

I've met a handful of people who are bored, but most people are enthralled. Reading about it or attending presentations on the ship help you appreciate the marvelous engineering achievement that it is, the cost of human lives in building it, and the importance to global shipping.

There are three sets of locks and the procedures for going through each is pretty much the same. But it's still fun to be on deck watching 50,000 tons of ship rise and fall as rainforest runoff powers the motion. I love that juxtaposition of the engineering marvels and heavy equipment next to a couple of guys in a dinky rowboat who pass the lines from ship to shore.

Beside the lock mechanisms to marvel at, there are several dredges in the canal. And, there is a steady stream of ships going the other direction.

Five million years ago there was no Isthmus of Panama. There was an oceanic seaway between North and South America. Volcanos generated by colliding tectonic plates created a bridge between the two continents and shut the seaway. And that changed everything.

Animals and plants from each continent tried their luck in expanding into the lands now open to them. Some were successful. This abrupt opening of a land bridge between the two continents, each with their successful ecosystems, led to migrations and extinctions. Armadillos, porcupines, opossums and dozens more travelled north and survived. Bears, otters, and wolves succeeded in expanding their range southward. This is the Great American Interchange.

A ship has moved out of the lock and the lock gates are starting to close. Photo by Charles Ford.

The closure of the seaway also had huge impacts on marine life and global climate. By re-ordering ocean circulation and initiating the Gulf Stream in the Atlantic Ocean, the isthmus changed the distribution of heat in the ocean. This allowed the Arctic Ocean to freeze. Only now, millions of years later are we seeing the Arctic return to its former ice-free self.

Lecturers rarely mention the wildlife you can see in the Canal. There are some 546 species of birds, over one hundred reptiles, 80 amphibians, and over 200 species of mammals. It will take great eyes and binoculars to see any, but on deck someone will offer you a glimpse through their binoculars if you don't have them.

At each end of the canal magnificent frigate birds circle high overhead. These are the robber barons of the bird world, stealing fish from other birds. The frigates save flight energy by using rising air, thermals, to gain altitude at the end of the land.

Near the Pacific end of the canal you might notice dozens of ring-tailed (or South American) coati on the starboard side if you're transiting from the Atlantic to Pacific. These are relatives of the raccoon, but larger. You can see their ringed tails held high as they walk through the grass on shore.

Between Gamboa and the Centennial Bridge we always see American Crocodiles lounging on the beach. The channel is narrow here so you are close to shore and able to see them. The crocs can be hard to see with their dark bodies on dark sand, but we always see them. There are also Spectacled Caiman. If you get a good look or photo you can tell them apart. If you see teeth, it is a Caiman. The crocs are also about twice as large when fully grown.

There are sloths in the trees and I've heard people say they see them, but I have not. Same for Spider monkeys and White-headed Capuchin monkeys.

There are lots of birds here. Two that stand out even for non-birders are the Brown Pelican and the Blue-footed Booby. A few more: Herons, Cormorants, and Red-billed tropic bird. The tropic bird is easy to identify with its crazy-long tail.

Kiel Canal

Longer than the Panama Canal, the Kiel Canal takes less time to navigate. The canal saves 250 miles of travel you would otherwise have to do to get around the Jutland peninsula. It allows passage between the Baltic Sea and the North Atlantic Ocean.

The flying ferry crosses the Kiel Canal without touching the water. Suspended from the Rendsburg bridge the ferry carries people and bicycles. Photo by Rod Brown.

Only medium and smaller ships can use the Kiel Canal. Larger cruise ships are too tall to go under the several bridges.

There is an entrance and exit lock at the ends, but no other locks. The land on either side is flat and pastoral. You pass by villages and towns and pass under seven highway bridges. The high bridge at Rendsburg has something you want to photograph.

The Kiel Canal has locks at each end, but none elsewhere. The surrounding land is flat farmland with towns and villages. Photo by Rod Brown.

The Kiel Canal offers bucolic views and a shorter passage between the Baltic Sea and the North Sea. Photo by Barbara Sobey.

The surrounding land is so flat and the bridge is so tall (to allow ships to pass under it) that the bridge approaches stretch nearly 5 miles from one end to the other. Obviously that would be a long way to walk or ride a bike to cross the canal. So there is a ferry. The ferry is suspended beneath the bridge. It doesn't float on the water; it floats above the water. It is called a "transporter" bridge.

Suez Canal

The Suez Canal was completed in 1869 by the same man, Ferdinand de Lesseps, who started building the Panama Canal. Suez, unlike Panama, doesn't have to take ships up and over a mountain range and hence has no locks. This made the construction much easier and cheaper. Even so it took ten years with much forced labor to complete the 120 mile long canal. Competition from the newly enlarged Panama Canal drove Egypt to expand the Suez Canal in 2015. It can handle larger ships and more ships than the Panama Canal can.

It is pretty weird to be sailing through sand dunes populated by the occasional camel. There are

also towns, industrial faculties, war memorials, mosques, and farms to see along the way. There is one bridge, the Mubarak Peace Bridge that crosses the canal, linking Africa to the Arabian Peninsula.

Desert lands surround you on a voyage through the Suez Canal. Photo by Peter Devine.

There is a big ecological story here with this no-lock canal. For one hundred years the Great Bitter Lake and Small Bitter Lake in the middle of the canal prevented species from crossing through the canal. The hyper saline waters of the lakes were toxic to most marine life. Red Sea species stayed at home as did Mediterranean species. But over the decades as the salinity of the lakes equalized with seawater, they became less bitter and species began moving through.

Today some 300 Red Sea species have invaded the Mediterranean. Surviving in the less rich and higher salinity waters of the Red Sea has apparently made them heartier. A few Mediterranean species have invaded the Red Sea, but not many. The Med was an ecological mess with

Left over from World War II these odd forts decorate the lower Thames River.

over-fishing and pollution before the invasion of foreign species. Now, it's much worse.

The Bermuda Triangle

Cue the scary music. There have been so many shipping disasters and aircraft loses in this area that it has taken on a reputation of danger. The triangle vertices are Bermuda, San Juan Puerto Rico, and Miami.

Airplanes go down with no apparent cause. Ghost ships wander into the triangle. All manner of marine disasters occur here.

However, comparable types of marine disasters also occur everywhere else throughout the ocean. They occur within the Bermuda Triangle at no greater frequency than anywhere else. Lloyd's insurance does not charge a premium for a ship to pass through the triangle. You know they would

charge more if they thought the liability was higher.

It turns out that some good creative writing coupled with a loose interpretation of events thrown onto a gullible public created the Bermuda Triangle hub-bub. Nearly all the incidents attributed to mysterious forces in the Bermuda Triangle have plausible causes. Some do not. But there are lots of other mysterious events in all the areas of the world ocean. There is nothing special here.

So what you won't see sailing across the Bermuda Triangle are ships sinking and planes dropping into the ocean. With some nice weather you might see a marlin, tuna, Sargassum weed, and flying fish.

The Maunsell Forts

One thing we were not expecting to see sailing in Thames estuary were remnants from World War II. To our surprise we found the Maunsell Forts at Shivering Sands. Although decommissioned in the late 1950s the forts were not removed. People have used them for time to time, but today they are abandoned.

Our experience seeing the Maunsell Forts is the reason we travel. The world is filled with wondrous things man-made or created in nature. We get to enjoy them only when we step outside our usual surroundings and go looking. Cruising is one way to find them. I wish you good luck in making grand discoveries.

Index

The Author

Ed Sobey holds a Ph.D. in oceanography and teaches oceanography and meteorology for *Semester at Sea.* He also lectures at sea for passengers on several cruise lines and has traveled the equivalent of ten times around the world at sea. Ed is a Fellow of The Explorers Club and has participated in two dozen scientific expeditions. He is a former naval officer and has directed five science centers, received two Fulbright specialist grants, published 31 books, and hosted two television series. Ed also founded the National Toy Hall of Fame.

Lightning Source UK Ltd.
Milton Keynes UK
UKHW051918140122
397169UK00003B/27